GAS DEBT AND DISCONNECTIONS

The Policy Studies Institute (PSI) is Britain's leading independent research organisation undertaking studies of economic, industrial and social policy, and the workings of political institutions.

PSI is a registered charity, run on a non-profit basis, and is not associated with any political party, pressure group or commercial interest.

PSI attaches great importance to covering a wide range of subject areas with its multi-disciplinary approach. The Institute's 50+ researchers are organised in teams which currently cover the following programmes:

Family Finances – Employment – Information Policy – Social Justice and Social Order – Health Studies and Social Care – Education – Industrial Policy and Futures – Arts and the Cultural Industries – Environment and Quality of Life

This publication arises from the Family Finances programme and is one of over 30 publications made available by the Institute each year.

Information about the work of PSI, and a catalogue of available books can be obtained from:

Marketing Department, PSI
100 Park Village East, London NW1 3SR

Also available from PSI

CREDIT AND DEBT: The PSI Report (Richard Berthoud and Elaine Kempson)

Three concerns dominate the debate about household finances in the 1990s: the increasing gap between rich and poor; the rising use of consumer credit; and the growing number of households in debt.

Richard Berthoud and Elaine Kempson have carried out the first ever survey of credit and debt. Their report provides new experience about household spending, consumer credit and debt.

229 x 150 mm, 320 pp, hardback, ISBN 0 85374 497 1, £24.95

Gas Debt and Disconnections

Karen Rowlingson and Elaine Kempson

POLICY STUDIES INSTITUTE
London

The publishing imprint of the independent
POLICY STUDIES INSTITUTE
100 Park Village East, London NW1 3SR
Telephone: 071-387 2171 Fax: 071-388 0914

© **Policy Studies Institute 1993**

ISBN 0 85374 585 4

PSI Research Report 751

A CIP catalogue record of this book is available from the British Library.

1 2 3 4 5 6 7 8 9

PSI publications are available from
BEBC Distribution Ltd
P O Box 1496, Poole, Dorset, BH12 3YD

Books will normally be despatched within 24 hours. Cheques should be made payable to BEBC Distribution Ltd.

Credit card and telephone/fax orders may be placed on the following freephone numbers:

FREEPHONE: 0800 262260
FREEFAX: 0800 262266

Booktrade representation (UK & Eire):
Book Representation and Distribution Ltd (BRAD)
244a London Road, Hadleigh, Essex SS7 2DE

PSI subscriptions are available from PSI's subscription agent
Carfax Publishing Company Ltd
P O Box 25, Abingdon, Oxford OX14 3UE

Laserset by Policy Studies Institute
Printed by Bourne Press Ltd, Bournemouth

Acknowledgements

We would like to thank the interviewers who worked on this study for all the effort they put into it: Jane Malone and Jan Lecluse in British Gas region North Thames, Chris Jacobs and Marie Kennedy in East Midlands and Jill Hearn in Northern. The fieldwork was far from easy as customers were not only difficult to contact but were widely dispersed geographically. The low level of refusals and the extent of the information we have even about the people we failed to contact is a tribute to their skills as interviewers.

We are also very grateful to all the respondents who gave their time to this study. Pseudonyms are used throughout the report to protect their anonymity. For many, it was painful to talk about the serious difficulties that they had recently faced. We hope that this report can in some way improve the situation in the future for people in their positions.

And last, but not least, we would like to thank British Gas for sponsoring this study. The report will not make easy reading for the sponsors, but we are confident that their commitment to this fully independent research will be matched by an equal commitment to deal with the issues raised.

Contents

Introduction

Gas disconnections peaked at 60,778 in 1987. In the next two years, the number declined drastically to 19,379 and stabilised at around 19,000 a year until it fell to 15,707 in 1992. With 16.9 million British Gas customers, the proportion of disconnections is small – less than one customer in every thousand. However, that anyone is disconnected *at all* is an issue of concern for British Gas and consumer groups alike.

The aim of this research was to investigate why the fall in the number of disconnections has levelled off. The question breaks down into two parts. First, why people originally get into debt and secondly, why this debt sometimes leads to disconnection.

While there has been a great deal of research into the reasons for fuel debt, the issue of disconnection has received less attention. Until now it has been claimed that most disconnections occurred because customers did not get in touch with British Gas. For example, in the quarter ending December 1992, 3,926 disconnections took place. In 62 per cent of cases there was no contact and in 34 per cent of cases, contact had broken down, according to British Gas figures. This study therefore set out to investigate non-contact as a way of understanding the reasons for disconnection.

Forty five British Gas customers were interviewed in depth. Most (39) of these had got into arrears and 33 of them had ended up disconnected. They were selected to give a range of different circumstances:

- people who had set up payment plans and avoided getting into arrears
- people who had set up repayment plans after getting into arrears and had avoided disconnection
- people who had set up payment plans and were subsequently disconnected
- people who had contacted British Gas within two weeks of disconnection and reached a payment agreement
- people who did not contact British Gas after disconnection.

There are considerable regional differences in the proportions of customers disconnected and in the statistics on non-contact. So interviews took place in three of the British Gas regions. These were Northern, East Midlands and North Thames. The first two of these have disconnection rates which are about the average for the country as a whole; while the level in North Thames is double the national average.

Although we achieved the 45 interviews we planned, we faced difficulties contacting the customers. Twenty-six households could not be contacted for one reason or another. Sixteen people were known to have moved away and a further ten were away for an extended period. Some were working abroad – one was working on an oil rig, another was an opera singer on a tour of Europe – others were away on long trips.

It was not easy to find people at home and our interviewers often had to make repeated calls at different times of the day and week. This is an important finding in itself since British Gas are obliged to make only one personal call on debtors and this tends to take place in office hours during the week. If our interviewers had adopted that approach, we would not have had a study to report on.

The interviews were designed to provide a detailed understanding of the reasons why people fell behind with their payments for gas, how British Gas debt recovery procedures worked from the customer's point of view and why some people failed to avoid disconnection. The structure of the report reflects these objectives. Part I focusses on the reasons for people's gas debts and unravels some of the complex situations where a number of factors act together to cause difficulties. Part II looks at the processes of debt recovery experienced by the families we interviewed. In doing this it tries to uncover the reasons why the set procedures fail to avoid disconnection, as well as describing the experience of the disconnection process and living long-term without gas.

The names and addresses of people for interview were selected by staff at the three regional offices to our precise specifications. Steps were taken, however, to ensure that British Gas would not be able to identify the people in the study. This, of course, means that it was not possible to check British Gas records to get their version of events and so this report is based solely on the accounts of their customers. While information from the records would have been very interesting, the confidentiality of the interviewees had to be protected.

Key findings

Gas debt

While there is a well-established relationship between low income and fuel debt, the relationship is not a simple causal one. For example, not all those on low incomes have fuel arrears and not all those with arrears are on a low income. This study explains how low income is related to fuel debt.

- It is difficult for people living long-term on social security to survive without getting into debt. Any sudden changes in their lives such as moving house or storm damage can cause even greater difficulties.
- Loss of income through unemployment can lead to particular problems in cases where:
  - People receive only hardship payments because they are deemed 'voluntarily unemployed'
  - People receive hardship payments while the DSS sorts out their benefit claim
  - People delay their benefit claims
- Some people in low-paid jobs have lower incomes than they would have on Income Support. This is partly due to non take-up of Family Credit. Only two of the eight families eligible for Family Credit in the study were claiming it and both these had avoided debt. Only two eligible non-claimants had also avoided debt.
- Others in low paid jobs are not entitled to Family Credit either because they do not have children or they are earning just a little too much. High mortgage repayments sometimes leave them with very little disposable income and therefore increase the likelihood of debt.
- Changes in circumstances, such as divorce or illness, can cause great disruption to the household finances of people on low incomes which again increases their risk of debt. Even those on a higher than average income may find it difficult to cope with their financial commitments when they are going through emotional difficulties.

Not all those in the study were on a low income. Some were earning higher than average wages. They tended to get into debt because of poor money management and absence from home on business.

Other reasons for debt included difficulties with payment methods and unexpectedly high bills. One customer was convinced that British Gas had mistakenly disconnected him instead of the squatters who lived next door.

Evidence of people who were 'working the system' was fairly weak. Only two people understood the process of debt recovery well and had deliberately not paid on time.

Gas debt recovery procedures and disconnection

In their document *Principles for the collection of domestic gas debt*, British Gas make a commitment that 'Disconnection of a gas supply will only take place as a last resort, when every other alternative has been exhausted'. These alternatives include payment plans, token meters and, where appropriate, direct deductions from social security payments – Fuel Direct.

Payment plans

Some people in debt do avoid disconnection by going onto repayment plans. It is often a struggle to repay the arrears and these people sometimes only narrowly avoid being cut off. Their success is generally due to fear of debt and disconnection.

Others, who set up repayment plans, still get disconnected. This is sometimes due to unrealistic levels of repayment and sometimes caused by mobility problems which prevent elderly or disabled people making the payments due. On occasions people facing difficulties keeping to their payment plans avoid contacting British Gas because they feel they cannot cope with the financial situation they are in. They are subsequently disconnected.

Many customers who live on low incomes make no attempt to negotiate a repayment plan because they have no money to offer and feel that British Gas can, or will, do nothing to help them. Although the literature sent out by British Gas early in the debt recovery process does mention alternative ways of paying gas bills, it does little to counteract the impression that arrears must be paid in full.

Better-off customers who fail to avoid disconnection by negotiating a payment plan usually do not get in touch because they are away from home for an extended period or are very disorganised about bill paying.

Prepayment meters

If they fail to negotiate a payment plan or a plan subsequently breaks down, gas customers should still be able to avoid disconnection if they request a token meter. Unfortunately, awareness of token meters is limited. The *Helpline Pack* is the main communication from British Gas which mentions the possibility. Some people are sure they did not receive a *Helpline Pack* or any other communications in which a token meter was mentioned. Those who are aware of token meters are not always keen to have one. Problems getting tokens was one of the reasons for this reluctance, but further research is needed in order to understand these attitudes more fully.

Some people are keen to have a meter, but are told by British Gas staff that they have to repay all their arrears first. One customer was told by her probation officer that she would have to be disconnected before she would be given a meter.

Fuel Direct

Arrears on fuel bills can be deducted at source from the social security payments of some benefit claimants. As with token meters, awareness of Fuel Direct is limited, people who are aware do not always want to go on the scheme and people who *do* want to go on the scheme are not always successful in doing so before disconnection. One customer was told by the Department of Social Security that he would have to be disconnected before he would be accepted onto Fuel Direct.

There are, however, other consequences for those paying off their arrears through Fuel Direct or a token meter. Where gas arrears are only one of a number of deductions being made from benefit, claimants are left with very small sums of money to live on. Those with pre-payment meters often find themselves too short of money to afford the fares to a gas showroom and the cost of tokens. As a consequence they are deprived of their gas supply.

Disconnection

Many people feel that British Gas is justified in principle to disconnect them because they were in arrears. But they are angry that their homes have been entered without permission. After disconnection, there is a view that British Gas staff are less sympathetic to them than they were before.

Reconnection

British Gas statistics show that about one in seven customers find the money to pay their debt and get reconnected within a month of disconnection. Some of these had the money all the time, but were away from home or unaware that they were in arrears. Others, particularly those with children, struggle to find the money because they feel they have to get their gas supply reconnected. They generally find the money by borrowing from friends or relatives or getting into debt with other commitments.

Others manage to get reconnected because they accept a token meter or go onto Fuel Direct. Some of these had asked for Fuel Direct or a meter before disconnection, but either asked too late or the Department of Social Security took too long to prevent disconnection. Others did not want to pay for their gas in this way and only accepted it because they needed to restore their gas supply.

Long-term disconnection

Most people, however, remain disconnected for more than a month. A proportion of these are away from home long-term or have moved away completely. Some, however, decide to live without gas, even if they were heavily dependent on it. This is usually because they continue to believe that there is no point getting in touch with British Gas if they have no money to offer. In some cases, they have contacted British Gas in the past without any success and so feel there is no point trying again.

Part I

GAS DEBT

1   A profile of gas debtors

Fuel debts are strongly associated with low incomes and financial hardship. This was the conclusion of a number of earlier studies and still seems to be true in 1992.

In *Fuel debts and hardship*, Richard Berthoud reported on a survey of 2,000 fuel customers, 650 of whom had been disconnected. The main conclusion was that low income rather than over-expenditure was the cause of arrears. But not all people on low incomes had fuel debts (particularly elderly people) and not all people with debts were poor. So although low income was highly correlated with debt, the relationship was not a simple causal one. Other factors, such as fear of debt and disconnection, poor money management or deliberate late payment also played a part.

The link between debt and disconnection was also a more complex relationship than it first seemed. Not all of those in debt were subsequently disconnected and regional board policies were an important factor here. One region implemented a deliberate policy to stop disconnections but had to abandon this when the level of debt rose greatly, implying that, for some people, disconnection was a deterrent to getting into arrears. This highlights an important dilemma for fuel companies. If they disconnect early in the debt recovery process they are accused of depriving people of their supply for the sake of a small amount of money owed. On the other hand, if they disconnect late, they are criticised for allowing a bill to mount up. This is, perhaps, one reason for the attempt to distinguish between 'won't pays' (who will be threatened with disconnection at an early stage) and 'can't pays' (who will be given more time and more help to clear their debts). It is extremely problematic, however, to apply this distinction in practice (Berthoud, 1981).

The PSI report, *Credit and debt,* identified five key factors which stood out as being strongly correlated with debt.

Age: The younger people were, the greater the risk of debt. Pensioners had hardly any debt problems.

Family type: Families with children had a higher risk of debt than those without children. The more children there were, the greater the risk of debt.

Income: Debt was strongly associated with low income. It was also linked to unemployment.

Commitments: For households with moderate incomes, substantial commitments on household costs or credit repayments increased the risk of debt.

Money management: People who felt it was acceptable to delay payments were relatively likely to have debt problems. Similarly the approach to budgeting was important people who were not careful budgeters had an increased risk of debt.

The most striking finding of the research was the number of contributory influences on the risk of debt, and the complexity of the interactions between them. None of these factors led to a high risk of debt on their own. It was combinations of characteristics which led to problems. For example, poor couples without children, or better-off families with children had few debts. The problems were concentrated among poor families with children. The greater the number of high-risk factors that applied to a household; the greater was their risk of debt.

Generally speaking, there was little evidence that debt was linked to a consumer lifestyle. It was more clearly associated with the everyday problems of budgeting on a low income. This was especially true for those who had got into debt with their gas bills. The amount spent on fuel bills varied only marginally with income, so poorer households with less disposable income found fuel bills more difficult to pay. One in nine of non-pensioner households with net incomes of less than £100 per week had got into arrears with their gas bills.

When people were asked for their own explanations of why they had got into debt, it was clear that fuel debts were much more likely to be attributed to low incomes than were any other types of debt (Berthoud and Kempson, 1992).

It is clear from previous research that low income is an important factor in relation to fuel debt. By low income, we mean those solely or mainly reliant on social security for their income, or in low paid work with a total income below £200 a week. At present, a very significant proportion of families in Britain are solely or mainly reliant on social security. Four million families receive Income Support. These are mainly pensioners, lone parents and those who are unemployed. About 2.9 million people are recorded on the unemployment register, of whom 600,000 receive Unemployment Benefit. A further one million people receive Invalidity Benefit. There are also 450,000 families with children who receive Family Credit, the social security payment which tops up earnings for these working households.

3

Table 1   Explanations for fuel debt

			Percentages
	All debts	All fuel debts	Gas	Electricity
Insufficient income	25	33	36	31
Reduced income	26	15	17	14
Unexpected bills	10	18	17	19
Over-commitment	24	17	14	19
Withheld payment	4	6	8	5
Overlooked payment	5	4	6	2
Base : All problem debts	*484*	*78*	*36*	*42*

Source: R. Berthoud and E. Kempson, *Credit and debt*, Policy Studies Institute, 1992.

One reason for some people on low income getting into debt could be that benefit levels are not set high enough for them to be able to maintain even a basic standard of living. Recent studies have suggested that Income Support was not enough, even when claimants only receive it for a short time (Kempson, Bryson and Rowlingson, 1993, forthcoming, ACS Yu, 1992). The study carried out by York University claimed that Income Support payments for a family with two children were £36 a week below the level required to support a simple lifestyle, with no allowance for smoking, drinking or an annual holiday (Yu, 1992).

While the link between low income and fuel debt is well established, the relationship is not a simple causal one. The strength of qualitative research is that it can explore the interaction of other factors with low income which then increase the likelihood of debt (such as changes in circumstances, or overcommitment).

In common with other research like *Credit and debt*, the people we interviewed in this study who had gas arrears were mainly living on low incomes. More than a half of them relied on social security payments (*Income Support, Retirement Pension or Invalidity Benefit*) as their main source of income, or, in three cases, were eligible for benefit they had not claimed. A further one in five lived on low wages, in many cases very low wages and not claiming benefits they were entitled to. Only a quarter of the households with arrears had net incomes of more than £250 a week (Appendix 2 Table 3).

In fact, a large number of families were, or had been, living on incomes *below* the Income Support level. Two people were not entitled to full

Income Support because they had been deemed 'voluntary unemployed'. One was unsure of his position because he took voluntary redundancy, but he was not receiving any benefits and his redundancy money had already run out. Another received hardship payments when he was first made redundant while the Department of Social Security sorted out his claim for Unemployment Benefit. All four were therefore living below Income Support levels because they were not entitled to any more money.

There were also many cases of people not claiming the benefits to which they were entitled and therefore living on incomes below Income Support. One young man was not claiming Income Support. He was surviving through reliance on other members of his extended family. There was also a woman who was not claiming any benefits even though she may have been entitled to Unemployment Benefit. When two men saw their businesses collapse, they both delayed claiming benefits until they had virtually nothing to live on. Another household should have been claiming Family Credit and was living on less than Income Support due to the extremely low wage of the sole wager earner.

The disposable incomes of some families were extremely low due to their mortgages. In some cases, they had less disposable income to live on than they would have had if they were claiming Income Support.

Compared with the population as a whole they included fewer pensioners than might have been expected and fewer couples without children. At the same time lone parents were somewhat over-represented. Again this was exactly in line with the characteristics of the PSI study *Credit and debt* (Appendix 2 Table 5). But whereas the *Credit and debt* survey showed that debts tended to be associated with younger age groups, the people we interviewed who had gas arrears and those who had been disconnected were more likely to be in their middle-age (Appendix 2 Table 4). People from ethnic minorities were also over-represented compared with the total population of Britain, but this probably just reflects the fact that ethnic minorities are disproportionately represented in low income groups (Appendix 2 Table 6).

The earlier study, *Fuel debts and hardship*, identified significant proportions of households who were considered 'at risk' who had been disconnected from their gas supply. These were families with babies under one year old, with children under school age and people who were sick or disabled. Nearly half of families fell into one of these categories (Berthoud, 1981). This still seemed to be a problem ten years later, with about one in four of the families in arrears containing a very young child or someone who was sick or disabled.

For two-thirds of the households, gas arrears were not the only financial problem they faced and 16 of the 39 households who had gas bill arrears, also had arrears on at least two other commitments. In almost all cases these were debts on other household bills: poll tax, not paid by nearly a half of the 39 households, electricity, water rates or mortgage. Consumer credit was not used to any large extent by most households and only three of them had got into arrears with credit commitments.

In subsequent chapters we look in detail at not only the circumstances but the main contributory factors to households getting into arrears with their gas. In particular, since so many people were claiming social security or living on very low wages, we explore whether low incomes alone are sufficient explanation of why some people get into difficulties, or whether there are other contributory factors. Other possible explanations such as patterns of budgeting, people being away from home, administrative difficulties with gas payments and deliberate non-payment are also examined, in particular to see whether they offer an explanation for the arrears run up by the quarter of households who were not living on either social security or low wages.

In this study, we interviewed 45 people, but in one household there were four nuclear families which each count as a benefit unit. We therefore have details of 48 family units. Of these, six had not been in arrears. This part of the report will therefore focus on the 42 families who were in fuel debt.

2   Long-term benefit claimants

For some people, living on a low income over a long period of time was enough, on its own, to lead them into debt. This was particularly true of those living on Income Support.

Len's situation was bleak. He was interviewed by a very experienced interviewer who had worked for PSI on a number of studies as well as for other organisations. Her description of his home is poignant:

> *The house inside was the worst I've seen in my work ... it was so desolate. For one thing, it was very cold; that deep chill that comes from being never warm. It was colder inside than it was outside, and that was saying something because it was sleeting and snowing outside ... Everything was so dark and gloomy ... I haven't felt the rigours of poverty so closely anywhere else I've been for you (or anyone else I've worked for) and I've seen some pretty down-trodden places down the years.*

Len was 45. He was unmarried and his parents were no longer alive. He lived alone in a council house sparsely furnished with worn out 1950s furniture (no TV, video or midi system here). He had had no job of any description for two years and had not had what he called a 'serious job' for 14. This kind of extremely long-term unemployment may be fairly unusual, but government figures released recently showed that one third of all those unemployed (about 1 million) had been without work for at least a year. Despite the difficulties of finding a job, Len had not lost his hope or sense of humour and still put all his effort into finding work:

> *The root of my problem is to get myself a regular job ... I've never wanted a lot ... I live on me own, I've got to live on me own, cos I can't get involved with any lady, cos I've got nowt to give her!*

But it was not easy to keep cheerful:

*I've had 14 years of this. Where's it going to end? I'm 45
now, am I going to be 65 until I start getting a pension, if I'm
going to get a pension? I haven't worked full-time for 14 year.
I've got another 20 year to live yet – working life. What's going
to happen?*

Len received £69.40 a fortnight in Income Support, after deductions for
poll tax and water rates. After paying other bills, Len liked to make sure
he had enough money to travel around in search of work. He was very
careful with his money:

*I try and save a bit; even if it's only going to last me a week.
Surprising what you can do with two or three quid.*

But Len did not feel he was managing well and wished that
organisations like British Gas understood his situation:

*It's getting me down. If they can take into consideration, I've
nearly had 14 years of having no work and living on this.
Situation I'm in now, how the hell can I be [managing well]?*

Now that winter had arrived, Len's lack of gas supply was making
matters even worse:

This is no good. It's depressing enough without this.

Len got into arrears when he received his last winter quarter bill for
£150. He asked to pay this in instalments but the £15 a week requested by
British Gas amounted to about half his income.

Ben's car repair business collapsed in 1989. At the time of the
interview, he was taking a HND/BTech in Business Studies to help him
start up in business again. In the meantime, he was living on Income
Support of £165 a fortnight along with £100 a month Child Benefit. Ben
shared responsibility for his three children (aged 15, 13 and 11) with his
ex-wife – they had a one week on/one week off rota. He found it much
easier to manage money when he had his business going. He put his
children first and although he was on a low income, found it difficult to
deny them things – 'You can't say "no"'.

Ben's arrangement with his ex-wife for sharing the care of their
children could cause difficulties for the Department of Social Security in
determining how much he should receive in Income Support. The social
security system is often thought to be complicated at the best of times, but
it is simplest with nuclear family structures – a single person, a couple, or
a couple with children. When families do not conform to these ideal types,
the benefit system is even more complex. From the amount Ben was

receiving, it seems that he was claiming for the children virtually all the time, or coming to some arrangement with his ex-wife. Even so, after three years on Income Support, he had now lost the battle against debt.

Wendy lived in the North East and had had a turbulent life despite being only 22. When she was 20, Wendy gave birth to her third child and had to stay in hospital for three months while her social worker found her a council flat. The baby's father was dead and her two other children from a previous relationship lived with her mother. Wendy was on probation for shoplifting and had been warned that she would go to prison if she was caught again. For two years, she had received Income Support of £46 a week (after deductions) along with £11.25 a week One Parent and Child Benefit – her mother took the rest for the two other children. Wendy said that her baby was her top priority – buying nappies and keeping the place warm. She found it difficult to manage her money:

> *It gans [goes] newhere. Soon as I get paid, I'm skint again.*

She had arrears on gas, electricity, rent and poll tax. She was having money deducted from her benefit for rent and electricity arrears. She had a gas token meter, but did not always have enough money for it as she was dependent on gas for heating, hot water and cooking, and so used a great deal. Sometimes she stayed with friends when she could not afford to keep herself and her baby warm. Another tactic she used was to heat up water in her electric twin tub and then use that for her baby's bath. In order to make ends meet, Wendy bought stolen goods from her friends who had shoplifted them. Despite the warnings of probable imprisonment, Wendy felt that she would have to return to shoplifting at Christmas in order to provide presents as well as essentials for her three children.

Percy was 61 and lived in Sheffield. He used to be a sheet steel polisher, but had been unemployed for 14 years (the same length of time as Len). Percy received £53.71 a week. He called this benefit 'Unemployment Benefit', but people are only eligible for Unemployment Benefit for one year after being made unemployed. They would then, if eligible, go onto Income Support. But the money Percy said he was receiving is too high to be Income Support (which would be £42.45 a week). It is therefore likely that he was receiving Invalidity Benefit.

Invalidity Benefit (IVB) is more generous than Income Support for many people. And whereas eligibility for Unemployment Benefit is limited to a year, there is no time limit on claiming IVB. Nevertheless, Percy received his benefit on a Thursday and said that most of it had gone by Saturday. He paid £3.60 a week on his rent and water rates (after housing benefit), £7.50 a week for electricity, £15 a week on cigarettes and £5.60 a month on poll tax. Before he was disconnected he paid £40 a quarter for his gas. The rest of his money went on food and household items. His top priority was his rent and his lowest – cigarettes.

Although Percy admitted that he could just about cope from day to day on this income, he felt that it was not really enough. He could not save any money and found it difficult to allocate money to particular things. Percy could just about manage to avoid debt when there were no sudden costs to meet, but problems arose when there were changes to his otherwise orderly life.

Four years ago Percy was forced to move out of his council flat to make room for participants in the Student Games which his town hosted. He was given £500 as compensation for the move, but this did not cover the removal cost and the extra costs of buying new carpets, curtains and furniture. Percy's new home was a maisonette. It was larger than his previous flat and cost more to heat. He applied for a loan from the Social Fund to help pay for curtains and floor covering and was lent £300, which he then paid back at £5 a week. Having paid that off, he applied for another loan and was appealing against his application being turned down. Although Percy had been on a low income for a considerable time, it was the disruption caused by his enforced move which caused difficulties. Four years later he was only just emerging from them.

Audrey had also received Invalidity Benefit for some time and she currently received about £58 a week. She used to find it difficult to manage on this income, getting into arrears with her gas, and was very pleased when she qualified for Mobility Allowance three years ago (£121 a month) and Attendance Allowance (£28 a week) one year ago. She felt that these had made all the difference and she now had a reasonable standard of living.

Brenda was 64 and one of three pensioners who were interviewed. Her only income was the state pension of £55 a week which she had received for four years. She lived in a flat in sheltered accommodation, with her mother (who was in her 80s) living in the flat below. Brenda found it difficult to manage on her income, even though she budgeted carefully on a weekly basis. Brenda found it particularly difficult to find money for her water rates, as she could not pay them weekly. In order to pay off her water rates bill, Brenda borrowed money from a money lender. She knew that the interest rate was high (she thought it was about 60 per cent but it is almost certainly a great deal higher), but she was desperate for the money. She felt that she was getting into a cycle of debt – taking out further loans to pay off previous ones:

> *In fact, I have borrowed money to pay, like, different bills, like.*
> *What gets me is the water – the water bill is terrible and I*

always get caught up with that – and there's no way you can kind of pay that weekly so then I have to borrow off, like, the company. So you're all the while in a vicious circle.

Brenda went to the money lender for a £50 loan to pay her water rates:

I said I wanted about fifty pound to put to me money to put the water right. So he said I'd have to have another hundred and fifty, pay the hundred to them to finish me other one off, and leave me fifty, yeah. And then I'd be paying [£5 a week] another twelve month ... I wish I'd never started that.

Generally, Brenda felt that:

I get into difficulties sometimes, but I just seem to manage to keep scraping by.

Like Percy, Brenda could just about manage most of the time, but when something happens which is outside her normal routine it is difficult to cope. Brenda explained the difficulty she faced when a storm recently damaged her TV aerial:

Well that really stumped me, you know. So me mum lent it me. Anything unexpected like that really, really does me. I can just manage each week paying me way how I am paying it, but nothing extra on the top.

Albert had been retired for some time. He was 77 and had a small income from an occupational pension (he used to work for the Gas Board). He received £56 a week from his state pension and £22 a week from his occupational pension, so he was on a higher level of income than Brenda. Albert felt that he managed his money well. His main problem was being unable to get out to pay his bills and so he relied on the help of his neighbours.

In contrast, Harry, who was 65, was relatively well-off even though he had been retired for a few years. On top of his basic state pension, Harry received an occupational pension of £125 a week and £6 a week income from his savings. Harry was not sure how much his basic state pension was, which probably indicates the extent to which it was important to him as a source of income. He lived with his sister who qualified in her own right for a state pension. Although Harry had a payment plan he was one of the six in the study who had not been in arrears with his gas bills.

3 Recent loss of earned income

We have seen how, for some people, their financial problems arose through living long-term on state benefits. In other instances difficulties stemmed from a sudden loss of earned income, on occasions causing them to live on an income below the level of Income Support payments.

Ineligible for Income Support

For a variety of reasons, some people are not eligible for full Income Support payments when they become unemployed. It is often difficult for them to cope with a drop in income to levels below Income Support.

Sid was a lorry driver earning £135 a week until he was made redundant in September 1991. While the Department of Social Security was sorting out his Unemployment Benefit entitlement, he was given hardship payments of £23.35 a week to live on. Although this was only temporary, it was at this stage that Sid fell behind with his bills. When his claim was eventually sorted out, he was given Unemployment Benefit of £46.10 a week. In comparison to Income Support, Unemployment Benefit is slightly more generous for single people. Despite this, it is still a low income and Sid found it difficult to get his finances straight while claiming. He felt that he was struggling to manage and could not afford to have any social life except sitting at home and watching TV.

Doug was 41 and admitted to being a heavy drinker and gambler. In September 1991 he got a job as a cleaner for a transport company, earning about £100 a week. This was his first job in seven years. In July 1992 he was sacked from this job for being drunk at work. Because he was classified by the Department of Social Security as 'voluntarily unemployed', Doug was not entitled to full Income Support. He received only £25 a week and believed that after six months he would be entitled to about £40 a week full Income Support. Doug would be the first to admit that he was not very good with money even when in employment, but living on £25 a week for six months would be extremely difficult for anyone. Doug said:

> *I don't like debts. I say 'I don't like debts', but I'm up to my eyes in debts! But I don't go out looking for them.*

He had electricity arrears which were the result of sub-letting to a friend who then refused to pay his share. He had £400 water rates arrears, £200 arrears on a mail order catalogue and owed two years poll tax charges for which he was soon due in court. Last, but not least, he had a £400 fine for driving without insurance. Doug admitted that he had accumulated these debts because he gambled, drank and could not manage money, but it is very difficult to see how he could possibly clear these debts while living on £25 a week. Direct deductions would be one method of ensuring some debts were paid, but any deductions from £25 a week would leave Doug with very little indeed. He summed up his money management as:

> *You make what you buy last you. I mean, I'm a terrible gambler. I might buy a little grub, sometimes I buy a load, you know, and just sit here and watch the telly or something. Other times I'll go to the bookie's and probably blow the lot and just scrounge about on a fiver for a couple of weeks, or something like that.*

John was a single man in his 50s whose only companion was a friendly Alsatian. He was a nervous man with a stammer who found it difficult to do things for himself, relying heavily on the support and advice of a community worker. John used to work as a hospital porter and initially earned about £135 a week, including overtime. Due to stress at work (he said the hospital was understaffed), he was often having time off sick with high blood pressure. This meant that he lost £30 a week overtime money.

After many sickness bouts, he was persuaded by his union representative and a hospital manager to leave his job. He was then investigated by the Department of Social Security for voluntary unemployment and so was on reduced Income Support of £32.72 a week. Most of his rent was covered by Housing Benefit, but he spent £15 a week on tokens for his electricity prepayment meter – almost half his income – and owed £80 a month on a bank loan that he took out 'for everyday things' when he was working. At the time of the interview, he was disconnected from the gas supply and so had no cooking facilities or hot water (he did not even have a kettle). He went to the public baths to wash and bathe and visited friends to eat and sometimes ate out, although he knew that this was expensive.

In Gary's case, redundancy money made little difference to him. He was 28 and used to work as a fitter in a factory, earning about £180 a week. The firm was making people redundant and then asking remaining employees to work overtime. Gary refused to do this on principle.

Eventually Gary was offered voluntary redundancy. If he took this, he would receive some redundancy money, but he had only been there for three years so it would not be a great deal. But Gary knew that if he accepted the offer, he would not be entitled to Unemployment Benefit for six months because he would be classified as 'voluntarily unemployed'. If he refused the offer, Gary knew that at some time in the future he would be made redundant and the firm would not be able to afford any redundancy money – leaving him totally reliant on a very small amount of state redundancy money and then Unemployment Benefit. Gary weighed up the pros and cons of taking voluntary redundancy and felt that he was in a 'no-win situation':

> *I knew what was gonna happen, but I was given the old – the sort of situation where it's either take the voluntary now, or go with nothing later. Because the government's money's only a weekly wage for every year you've been there – I've only got three years. If you take the voluntary, you're not covered on your insurance for your mortgage and all that, so – it's a no-win situation. Because they say, 'Well – you've made – you've volunteered to be made redundant'. But there again if you get made redundant, you only get three weeks' wages, which is a pittance.*

Gary decided to take the redundancy money because he needed a lump sum to pay off his gas arrears. After a couple of weeks, the money was almost gone and Gary was living on his 23 year old girlfriend's Income Support of about £30 a week. After a further four weeks' unemployment he would be able to claim some benefit himself.

For Gary, redundancy money allowed him to pay off his gas debt, but it was not enough to cushion the blow of unemployment and taking voluntary redundancy adversely affected his benefit entitlement. Soon after taking redundancy, he was already having difficulty balancing his income with his outgoings:

> *You get into a situation where you have to start looking at remortgaging your house to start paying the bills. You have to borrow money – see friends, see relatives – 'if you can lend us a few quid' ... get by somehow.*

Eligible non-claimants of benefits

Sid, Doug, John and Gary were not eligible for full Income Support and so the drop of income following job loss was made even worse by the abysmally low benefit level they found themselves on. Others appeared eligible for benefits, but for various reasons did not claim them. Our calculations of benefit entitlement are based on detailed information from interviewees, but the study was not specifically designed to measure entitlement and so our findings give indications of entitlement, rather than wholly accurate measures.

Mavis was most likely eligible for Unemployment Benefit, but she was not claiming it. She was 53 and had worked in computer administration for a number of years earning about £90 a week. She had recently become unemployed but had not signed on. Mavis lived with Pete who earned about £100 a week as a supervisor with a cleaning firm. They paid £40 a week rent from their £100 a week income and so they were, clearly, not claiming the Housing Benefit to which they were entitled.

Mavis was very upset about her situation and was on anti-depressants:

> *I did start, you know, trying to put money aside. You dip into it when you're broke and you're hungry. You dip into it, you know, you need to ... The bills come in and they amount to about five or £600 at once, you know, and they want it now, and it just puts you in a panic.*

One method Mavis used to supplement their income, was to scavenge from local skips to find things that she and Pete may need. She was quite proud of this 'entrepreneurship'.

Sunil and Ray both knew that they were eligible for benefits when they became unemployed, but delayed their claim. Sunil's difficulties stemmed from the failure of his business and his initial reluctance to claim benefit. He used to run two shops, owned a car and was planning to buy a house, but then the business collapsed. The commercial landlord was still holding him to the terms and conditions of his lease and so Sunil owed £60,000. Ideally, he would have liked to start up another business, but he feared that the bank would declare him bankrupt, thus denying him the opportunity. Sunil was 33 and lived with his 22 year old wife and 2 year old son. After the failure of his business, he did not apply for any benefits for a few months. It was only when he had literally nothing to live on that he applied for and received Income Support of £138 a fortnight along with £38 a month Child Benefit. As he said:

> *First two or three months I didn't go to the Department of Social Security. I didn't work and I felt ashamed to go down there – a young man, going to sign on – well, really ... I lived on whatever I had ... I thought I would get a better job – something would get better or something would work out – and nothing worked out.'*

In order to get a foot in the employment door, Sunil took what was, for him, a fairly menial job – post and packing in a music shop. He worked for three hours a day (one hour in the morning and two in the afternoon). He took the job in the hope that the employers would eventually give him a full-time job:

> *I'm trying to learn it, you know. It's easy, but if I learn they might give me a full-time job.*

His 15 hours work a week affected his benefit entitlement, so that instead of receiving Income Support of £138 a fortnight, he received £105 a fortnight, along with his earned income of £28 a week. He was therefore only £11.50 a week better off for the 15 hours he works and this, of course, does not take into account the cost of travelling to and from work twice a day. Sunil was experiencing the unemployment trap whereby, financially at least, he was not much better off working than not working. But he found it difficult mentally to be unemployed and felt that although in the short term he may not be doing too well, in the long term he may get a full-time job. If he could work a few more hours a week, Sunil would come off Income Support and go onto Family Credit, probably making him and his family better off.

The experience of losing a business and being unemployed had various consequences for Sunil and his family – not merely financial:

> *I didn't work for some time. It really affected me mentally, because I lost all this money. It's very hard to make a business really.*

In March 1992, Sunil received his £80 gas bill. This was very soon after the business failure and both he and his wife were suffering from depression. He felt paralysed – unable to do anything about his situation.

Ray had a similar experience to Sunil. He and his wife ran a clothing franchise and were doing quite well for themselves until the recession hit and they lost the business in April 1991. They were declared bankrupt and were forced to take a second mortgage out on their home (£40,000 on top of the £47,000 mortgage they already had). Ray found a fairly low paid job quickly, in marketing, but he was struck by a second blow in June 1991 when his wife left him. One year later in June 1992, he was made redundant and had been unemployed since:

> *Well, everything went wrong for me, you see, because in April 1991, we went bankrupt; in June 1991, my wife left me; and from that point on I've had all the hassle with the house [subsidence]; and then in June this year I got made redundant.*

> *So just as things have started to get better, I've gone two step backwards.*

Like Sunil, Ray did not want to sign on:

> *See, that was something else I didn't do until the very last minute. I had a thing about signing on the dole. I wouldn't do it, cos I'd never been on before, so I had the pride and the principle. And when things got really bad, I had several friends who popped round and said, 'Well look, there are so many other thousands and millions of people who do it, there's no reason you shouldn't. You pay your dues into it, so when you come across hard times, you should be entitled to get something out.*

Ray signed on after about three months unemployment. Half his mortgage interest was eventually paid by the Department of Social Security, but this still left him to find £385 a month. By the summer of 1992, he had accumulated £9,000 mortgage arrears on his second mortgage and the house was on the market.

Low income prior to job loss

Previous research has shown that a large proportion of people who lose their jobs work in low-paid insecure jobs (Daniel, 1991). In such cases they often earn little more than they would get on social security, so that their financial position is very similar to people who live long-term on benefit.

Malcolm was 37 and until 5 months ago made eternity rings in a jeweller's shop. According to Malcolm, the boss disliked the fact that he was very quick to pick up skills and so sacked him. While he was in work, Malcolm was only earning about £75 a week. With this, he was supporting his wife and three children, including a newborn baby. Malcolm would have been eligible for Family Credit if he was working 16 hours or more a week. When he became unemployed, he received £71.45 a week Income Support payments on top of his Child Benefit. Despite being only £3.55 a week worse off on Income Support, Malcolm was not very happy with being unemployed and although he lived in the North, he had tried looking for work as far away as London:

> *Well to be quite honest, I don't like it, ' cos what we have is the barest minimum, you know. I wish I could do something about it – it's not for lack of trying. I've tried London, quite a few places in the South, Newcastle, all over. I'm trying to improve on it.*

Norman was not earning a great deal in his job as a joiner and when his £80 winter bill arrived in 1992 this coincided with his going on short-time working and so was difficult to pay. He had not managed to pay it all when he received his next bill of £50, by which time he was unemployed:

> *At the time I went out of work, the car insurance, electric, gas, all came together. One daughter's 21st, the other graduated – all just hit me in the one period of time. That was the time when it all came to a head.*

Norman could not even pass his time watching television as his set was broken and he did not have enough money to get it repaired, let alone buy a new one. He cut down on most things to save money. He tried to cut down on his gas consumption by having fewer baths. Norman found it painful to talk about his experiences in the last year and felt that:

> *I'm just staggering from one crisis to another.*

Toni had been receiving £56 a week Income Support along with £9.65 a week Child Benefit since the birth of her baby eight months ago. This was not a substantial drop for her as she had previously had casual jobs in pubs or factories, depending on availability. She had, therefore, been living long-term on a very low income and this was the root cause of her difficulties. Toni disliked debt greatly, but now that she had her baby, she put its needs first. Toni said she would get into debt if she thought it necessary to maintain an adequate standard of living for her baby. Fortunately for Toni, her mother was sometimes able to help her out when she got into difficulties.

4   Low paid work

Low income is not exclusive to those reliant solely on state benefits. People in low paid jobs may receive Income Support if they work fewer than 16 hours a week. If they work 16 hours or more and they have children, they could be entitled to Family Credit. Those without children who work more than 16 hours will not be entitled to any income maintenance benefits even though they may be earning a very small hourly wage. In such cases they are often on a similar level of income to those receiving social security.

Eligible non-claimants of Family Credit
Eligibility aside, people in work are not always aware of benefits like Family Credit without which, they may actually be *worse off* than they would be if on Income Support. Eight families out of the 42 in arrears relied on low-paid work for their income. Five of these were eligible to receive Family Credit, but had so far not claimed it. While most research on the subject emphasises that the majority of eligible non-claimants would only be entitled to small amounts of benefit, this was not the case with these five people. This reinforces the findings of a previous study which found a high correlation between mortgage arrears and non take-up of Family Credit. In fact, only 10 per cent of eligible claimants were receiving the benefit (Ford and Wilcox, 1992). Findings from another study, however, suggest that Family Credit claimants and eligible non-claimants have the same number of debts (Marsh and McKay, 1993, forthcoming)

Rosa was an eligible non-claimant of Family Credit. She earned £100 a week from her shop-cleaning job and £9.65 a week Child Benefit. She had an 11 year old daughter and so would have been eligible for about £35 a week in Family Credit on top of her income. After paying £38 a week rent, Rosa was left with only £71.65. This took her very close to what she would receive if unemployed and receiving Income Support. Rosa had recently applied for Housing Benefit which would help her. Her other bills were £44 a month poll tax, £40 a quarter electricity and £20 a month gas. Rosa felt she was 'just getting by' and she tried to put money away for all her bills, but it was not easy to manage on her income. Rosa's situation could be another difficult one for the benefit system as she spent two or three months a year in South America with her family.

Ibrahim's situation was more straightforward, but also more desperate. His problems stemmed from being made redundant twice in a short space of time. Ibrahim came to Britain thirty years ago from West Africa and took a degree in Electrical Engineering. He moved to London and had, until recently, always worked while in this country. In 1990 he was made redundant. He found another job quickly, working as a cleaner, but this job was on contract and ended in August 1991. Ibrahim had been out of work ever since.

When he became unemployed in August 1991, Ibrahim received Unemployment Benefit of £82 a fortnight. People are only entitled to spend one year on Unemployment Benefit, after which they may be able to claim Income Support. While entitlement to Unemployment Benefit depends on personal National Insurance contributions, entitlement to Income Support is means tested. Since Ibrahim's wife was working more than 16 hours a week, the family was ineligible for Income Support. This was confirmed when he appealed against the decision at a Social Security Appeal Tribunal.

This may not have caused problems if his wife had been earning a good income, but she was working as a dressmaker earning only £60 a week. A couple without children would be expected to live on this without any other benefits (except Housing Benefit and Community Charge Benefit), but Ibrahim had two children – aged 17 and 16. The family was therefore entitled to Family Credit of as much as £83.90 a week on top of the £60 a week his wife earned and the £56 a month they receive in Child Benefit. He was not told about this entitlement at the tribunal and, at the time of the interview, Ibrahim was still unaware of the existence of Family Credit and was trying to live on his wife's earnings and Child Benefit alone.

When Ibrahim was receiving Unemployment Benefit, the couple and their children were living on £114 a week, which he admitted was a struggle. Their outgoings included £46 a month for their mortgage, about £60 a month for their gas, £10 a week for their electricity, £13.75 a month for their water rates, £50 a quarter for their telephone bill and £90 a year for their poll tax. These bills alone worked out to £43 a week, a very large proportion of their income. Although Ibrahim tried to keep up all his payments, it is not too surprising, perhaps, that he had mortgage arrears of £900 and gas arrears of about £840, although he disputed the total amount of both of these. With an income of only about £75 a week, it is very difficult to see how Ibrahim could pay his current bills, let alone repay any of his arrears.

The situation of the Khan family was fairly complicated as they lived together as an extended family and shared income and outgoings to a certain extent. The social security system, however, does not generally assess households (Housing Benefit is the one exception) but treats each nuclear family separately. In order to understand the Khan household's situation, it is important to consider the whole household together even though the problems of each of the nuclear families differ.

Salim Khan was the 60 year old head of the extended family which lived in the London house they owned outright. Salim lived with his 55 year old wife, their three sons (aged 37, 21 and 18) and their three daughters-in-law (aged 35, 20 and 18). Along with these adults, lived Salim's seven grandchildren (aged 10, 9, 7, 6, 3, 18 months and 6 months). Although Salim's name was on the gas bill, he did not read or speak any English and so it was his eldest son, Tariq, who took responsibility for the bills since he spoke good English.

Salim was unemployed and he received £66.60 a week Income Support. For the seven children, they thought they received about £48 a week Child Benefit (but they probably received a little more than this). They also received £28 a week for one of the children who was blind, but they were unsure of the name of this benefit (it was probably Disability Living Allowance).

The four adult women in the household looked after their children and their home. They had no paid work and received no benefits, except Child Benefit. The largest part of the household's current income came from paid work. Two of Salim's three sons had paid jobs – working as sales representatives. Tariq earned £150 a week and his brother earned £120 a week. With four children, Tariq would have qualified for Family Credit. In fact he would probably have qualified for about £24 a week. His brother (with three children, but on a lower wage than Tariq) would probably have qualified for about £35 a week.

The youngest son was 18 and believed that he was only entitled to £3 a week Income Support and so, although he was unemployed, did not bother claiming. He may not have been entitled to Income Support when he was 17 (for example, if he was not on a training scheme), but once 18, he would certainly be entitled in his own right to £66.60 a week for himself and his wife. The three brothers were therefore failing to claim about £125 a week in social security payments.

At present, the family of eight adults and seven children were living on a total of £406 a week – equivalent to £27 per person per week. Their bills varied from £85 a week (when their bills were low) to £118 a week (when their bills were high). This left them with between £321 and £288 a week to feed and clothe eight adults and seven children and to buy any household items. The extra £125 a week benefit to which they were entitled would have made a substantial difference to their standard of living. But, like many families, the Khans did not work out their outgoings on a weekly basis and Tariq said that they were 'just surviving' on their current income. They never had enough money to put away for bills and so:

As soon as the bills come, we start worrying about it.

This was what they did in 1992 when they received their quarterly winter gas bill which was for £7-800. They felt that this was high, but this was partly because it was a winter quarter and partly because gas prices were going up. Tariq knew it would be a struggle to find the money, and they only succeeded after being disconnected.

In addition to these current non-claimants there were two further households which were in arrears with their gas bills and had been eligible non-claimants of Family Credit in the recent past. When Malcolm was working as a jeweller, he would definitely have been entitled to the benefit. Hannah's situation was more debatable and, once again, fairly complex. She received £60 a week from a lodger and earned some money from her art work. Her rent was paid by her ex-husband. Hannah's daughter had recently finished her A-levels and so was not dependent on Hannah any longer. But when she was dependent, Hannah had been living very close to the level of Income Support. If Hannah could have proved that she was working more than 16 hours a week, she may have been entitled to Family Credit. Income from lodgers is treated differently from 'earned' income and this would affect her entitlement to benefits.

Not all eligible non-claimants of Family Credit got into arrears. Two of the people interviewed had managed to pay their gas bills despite not claiming benefit they were entitled to. Deirdre was a lone parent, looking after her 14 and 12 year old children. She was entitled to (but not claiming) Family Credit of about £31 a week on top of the £85 a week she earned in her two part-time jobs and £60 a week in maintenance she got from her husband (the first £15 of maintenance is disregarded in any claim). She felt that she was managing quite well on her income:

I haven't got myself in no trouble!

Deirdre went onto a gas budget account about five or six years ago when she was with her husband and on a much higher level of income. When she first split up from her husband he paid no maintenance to her and she did get behind with her payments, but the money from him made all the difference now.

Ron, too, had avoided debt. Ron was 50 and was a lorry driver, earning £450 a month. He lived with his wife, Sheila, and their two children aged 9 and 8. They had also taken responsibility for their 2 year old nephew as his mother was in hospital and his father was unable to look after him. Ron's brother-in-law paid £20 a fortnight for the boy's upkeep. Taking into account only their two children and Ron's earnings, the family would have been entitled to about £36 a week Family Credit. They were also paying £23 a week rent and so may have been going without help from Housing Benefit.

Ron and Sheila kept out of debt by managing their money 'very carefully'. They were also very frightened of debt. They relied heavily on one of Ron's ex-employers, who acted as an informal adviser for help with budgeting. It was she who advised them to go on a gas Payment Plan. They were still 'terrified' of receiving large bills and 'threatening' letters.

Claiming Family Credit

The examples of Ron and Deirdre show that the failure to claim Family Credit entitlement is not invariably linked to debt. But it is interesting that the only two families who were claiming Family Credit had not been in arrears with their gas bills.

Viv was one of these. She was 36 and lived with her 6 year old daughter. She had separated from her husband in February 1992. At that time, she was ineligible for Family Credit because she worked 20 hours a week and the threshold for Family Credit was 24 hours. She began to claim Family Credit in April 1992 when the rules changed and received £149 every four weeks on top of her £92 a week earnings. Viv felt that she was much better off than when she had been with her husband even though, on paper, she appeared to have less money. He never gave her enough money and now she felt in control of her finances and her life. Viv received no maintenance from her husband and was thinking of taking him to court for it. If she was successful, she would lose 70 pence Family Credit for every pound she received over £15.

Hazel was 36 and had two school-age children aged 18 and 16. She was a nursery nurse for children with special needs and earned about £11,000 a year. She also received Child and One Parent Benefit totalling £124 a month as well as Family Credit of £133 a month. Part of this would stop when her 18 year old goes to college. Hazel's husband paid the mortgage (£340 a month) and she was one of the few people in the sample, apart from some of the very high earners, who managed to save money regularly. She saved between £150 and £200 a month.

Not eligible for Family Credit

Some people earn below-average wages and yet are not eligible for Family Credit, either because they have no children or because their incomes are just above the level at which they could claim. Those who rent their home may still qualify for help with their rent, but this is not the case for home owners, who must find all the money for their mortgage repayments. This can mean that their disposable income is very small.

Mike was earning £13,000 a year as an inspector for a transport company. The job was strictly '9 to 5' and so there was no opportunity to earn extra money by working overtime. This income (along with about £100 a month in Child Benefit) had to support Mike, his wife and their three children who were aged 11, 9 and 3. While the family were not entitled to Family Credit, they still found it difficult to manage on this income. Like the Khan family, they never managed to save up for a bill and struggled to find the money when they received one.

Two years ago Mike had been a driver with the company and had earnt up to about £22,000 a year by working overtime. Unfortunately, Mike discovered he had epilepsy and was consequently not allowed to work as a driver. Although he still had a job, the family was struggling on his reduced income. He earned slightly too much to qualify for Family Credit, but with the large mortgage he had (£950 a month), he may have been better off financially if he were unemployed and claiming Income Support or Unemployment Benefit when some of his mortgage interest would be paid. Mike was now very overcommitted and, in addition to his gas arrears, was eight months behind with his mortgage.

Gopal was 45 and worked as a payroll assistant for a utility company. He earned £790 a month which supported his wife and two children, aged 7 and 6. He was therefore earning too much to qualify for Family Credit. His mortgage repayments, however, were £590 a month and so he had little left over for food and any other household bills. In order to improve his situation, Gopal had taken in lodgers recently. Even so, he was about four months in arrears with his mortgage and had been disconnected from his gas supply.

Lisa and Mark did not have children, and at the time they got into arrears with their gas they were living on low wages, earning £11,400 a year between them. Out of this they had to find mortgage payments of £306 a month. Their joint income had recently risen to £17,900 and they were finding it much easier to cope with bills and other commitments.

Susanne and Tom were a newly formed couple in similar circumstances, living without children and on a low wage. Susanne was the main earner, working as a mobile hairdresser and earning between £100 and £150 a week. Tom had taken early retirement and currently worked as a taxi driver. He had not moved in permanently with Susanne and his contribution to the household budget was not clear, but was only a small amount of money. Susanne, too, had been disconnected from her gas supply and her home was currently up for sale.

5 Changes in circumstances

It is not easy for people to live long-term on low incomes or to cope with a large loss of income. This is particularly true when they suffer changes in circumstances which disrupt the pattern of their lives. A change in circumstances, such as moving home or becoming a lone parent can have serious adverse consequences for people on a low income. Family and employment changes can cause serious emotional difficulties which make any financial problems less easy to cope with.

Family changes

After he lost his business and his wife, Ray found it difficult to cope with things:

> *Well a lot of the time, you see, when all the emotions and things were around, you tend to lock yourself away. That's basically what I did, I just kept seeing people to try and get a job. And with one thing and another, you just hate people knocking on the door, and opening mail. Which, if anybody's honest, is a common factor, if anybody's been in that position.*

Malcolm was separated from his first wife eight years ago and took responsibility for the two children which came from that marriage. One year ago he married his current wife and moved into their present house. At that time, Malcolm was working in a jeweller's shop earning £75 a week. Five and a half months ago, Malcolm and his new wife had a baby. At this time, his 15 year old daughter from his first marriage went to live with Malcolm's sister, leaving his 9 year old son and the baby with him. Malcolm paid his sister £30 a week for looking after his daughter – a very large proportion of his income.

A couple of weeks after the birth of the baby, Malcolm was sacked from his job, but this did not reduce the family income very much as he was extremely low paid and had not been receiving Family Credit. He received no maintenance from his ex-wife as she refused to pay it. After paying his sister for his daughter's upkeep, Malcolm and his wife were left with £41.45

a week plus £17 a week Child Benefit to cover his 9 year old son and their young baby.

Wendy had led a turbulent life. At only 22, she had had three children. The father of the youngest was dead and Wendy's mother looked after the older two. Since the birth of her youngest 20 months previously, Wendy had had to start managing money for the first time. She did not find this easy on the money she received – £46 a week Income Support after deductions and £11.25 a week Child Benefit and One Parent Benefit. She found it much easier to manage when she was living with the father of her first two children.

Wendy had accumulated arrears with her rent, gas, electricity and poll tax. Money was deducted directly from her benefit to cover her rent and electricity while she had a token meter for her gas supply. She did not pay or worry about her poll tax bill (nor did she have a TV licence). Wendy bought items from her friends who shoplifted and although she is on probation for shoplifting herself, believed that she would have to go back to this at Christmas.

As far as Wendy's gas bills are concerned, she received a quarterly winter bill for £90 in 1992 and could not afford to pay it, 'so just left it'. This was the first bill that had caused serious problems as Wendy had saved her benefit while she was in hospital for three months with her baby, waiting for social services to find accommodation for her. But this money had run out and the baby was bigger – needing more nappies and newer clothes.

Nick had been a lone father for three years. He was 37 with two children aged eight and five. The period before the separation had been difficult for everyone involved. Nick said that his partner was an alcoholic who behaved unreasonably and irresponsibly. She had asked him to leave and, while he found the situation intolerable, he thought that if he left he might be denied contact with his children. So he stayed. Eventually she left, taking the family's Child Benefit book with her.

Although Nick was very glad to have responsibility for the children, he decided not to give up his job to look after them, but to employ a childminder instead. This was, of course, not without its costs. Nick earned £500 a week selling advertising space for a publishing company. He paid the childminder £120 a week, plus £60 a week for the children's food. He also paid £100 a week in taxi fares to take him and his children to and from the childminder and work. He also had a £750 a month mortgage. This left him with very little. Not surprisingly, Nick had huge debts, but he was determined that his children would not suffer and said that:

> *I'm doing all right. I earn a good living and I've been earning a regular good wage. I don't save money but the kids don't*

go short really ... My priorities are my children and their general welfare.

He also admitted, however, that he was not very good with money:

I drink it, gamble it and spend it. Me and money just don't mix.

On the day of the interview, Nick had just won £700 on the horses. He realised, however, that he lost just as much as he won.

Margaret lived in London but the rest of her family lived in Scotland. Due to serious health problems in her family, Margaret and her children had been spending a great deal of time there over the last seven months. Now that she was back in the South East, Margaret still worried a great deal about things in Scotland and found it difficult to be clear about what was going on in her life.

As well as recently being made unemployed, Norman also suffered a more personal loss. In 1979, Norman separated from his wife and he moved back to his mother. His mother died two years ago. At 44, Norman found this difficult to cope with and even now found it very painful to talk about these events. The loss of his job had been almost the last straw. Norman had relied first on his wife and then his mother to take care of all financial matters. At a time when he needed their emotional and practical help the most, there was no-one around.

Suzanne's business failed three years ago, as did her marriage a year later. Although Suzanne recovered from this enough to establish herself as a mobile hairdresser, she had always found it difficult to manage money. When she was married, there had always been enough money to pay their bills but, since her divorce, she had had to support herself and her daughter and things got more difficult. Her daughter, who was now 19 years old, had recently left home, which had helped financially. Suzanne had also met Tom who was giving her a lot of advice on how to manage her money.

Moving house

Along with family changes such as divorce, moving house also comes high on many stress indicators. For those on a low income, the accompanying financial effects can cause great difficulties. Percy, who had lived on benefit for 14 years, was forced by the council to move because his town was hosting the world Student Games. He went from a flat to a maisonette and so as well as removal costs, he had to find money for new carpets, curtains and other furnishings. Although he was given some help, the disruption made it difficult for him to avoid debt.

Moving house can have a particular impact on fuel debt. If someone moves to larger or less well insulated accommodation, they may find that their fuel bills are higher than they are used to. Percy certainly found that his gas bills went up in his new home.

Also, estimated bills will generally be based on the rate at which the previous occupants had used fuel and this may be higher than the present occupant. Margaret was a lone parent with three children living on Income Support. She moved into her new flat nine months previously. It was a conversion and was in poor condition. It was also an unfurnished flat and she needed to buy furniture and furnishings. She had only been in the flat for a total of two or three months, as the rest of the time the family had been in Scotland. When she came back from Scotland, she found that she owed £500 in gas arrears and had been disconnected. £500 worth of gas seems a great deal to have used in only two or three months, even though Margaret used it for her heating and hot water, and she queried the size of the bill. As she was away at the time the meter would have been read it seems likely that it would have been estimated on the basis of previous tenants' bills. But British Gas engineers are instructed to read meters when they go to disconnect a supply and should not disconnect if the actual reading is lower than an estimated bill.

Maxine moved into her council flat in November 1991. According to her, it was 'uninhabitable' and she lived with friends and relations while her brother helped her clean the flat and redecorate. The pre-war boiler was changed in December. Her bills were much higher than she felt they should be and it was only after the meter was changed in June 1992 that they fell to the level she felt reasonable.

Ill health

John's debt problems stemmed from when he was in work as a hospital porter. Due to under-staffing and a wish to earn more money, John worked long hours. This meant that he found it difficult to get to the gas showroom to pay his £10 weekly payments:

> I had no free time to do these things because I am responsible for so many things, you see, because I've got responsibility at work. The job I do, I have to be concentrated on that and on patients at work and stuff like this. You have got to be alert to know well what you mustn't do and things you must do. All these rules and regulations one has got to follow.

Although John was talking here in the present tense about his job, he did in fact take a lot of time off and eventually leave:

Once the pressure was too much – one just couldn't cope.

John's hours were reduced and although he had more time to get to the showroom, he had less money to pay his bill with. Likewise when he left the job. Apart from having obvious financial problems, John was also still suffering from stress:

With all the problems in my head I couldn't remember, I mean, what was going on ... Everything was getting out of hand.

John accrued gas arrears of about £140 and was disconnected. On an income of £32.72 a week he was not sure how he would be able to clear this. As well as his ill health, John felt that his age was another barrier to finding a job:

Once you're past fifty, you're asking the impossible.

6 Over-commitment

Previous research has shown that low income combined with high levels of commitment leads to a high risk of debt, especially in families with children (Berthoud and Kempson 1992).

When Gary was in work, he was earning £180 a week. This income supported him and his girlfriend, who was at college. Although this is a good deal more than people get on social security it is still a relatively low wage. Gary found it difficult to cope on it, especially when he decided to buy his house from the Housing Association he had previously rented it from. The mortgage was £280 a month (compared to a previous rent of £125 a month). He also found that he had to pay £900 a year service charges and ground rent. At the time of the interview, he had £700 mortgage arrears. Even if the housing market were more buoyant, Gary was not allowed to sell the house for another two years. Although unemployment undoubtedly made Gary's problems worse, he began to accumulate arrears while he was in work:

> *Anybody – any working man's struggling with bills. They tell me – everywhere I've worked, that – everyone's the same, like, when you talk about money. And every bill's a nightmare.*

Gary was clearly over-committed and the gas bill was not a major priority:

> *It's your priorities ... mortgage to pay, I've got food to buy ... and you have to put things in a list of priorities. If the gas or another one comes below that, then that's the one that suffers.*

Mike was having similar problems even though he was still at work. Mike's commitments dated from the time he was working as a driver, earning £22,000 a year with overtime. He had a large mortgage being repaid at £950 a month. A few years ago Mike and his wife took out a loan from a finance house to have double glazing. They still owed £1,600 on this. When he was diagnosed as epileptic Mike had to transfer to a lower paid job and his earnings dropped to £13,000. This is a very low wage with which to support a wife and three children, especially in view of his high level of commitments. Before he changed jobs he managed to keep up his mortgage repayments, but afterwards it became impossible. In the two years after he moved to his lower paid job, Mike accumulated 9 months of arrears on his mortgage (£8,550). Although Mike's credit cards had been taken away from him, he still owed £300. The local council claimed that Mike and his wife owed them £1,500 for their poll tax (although Mike disputed this figure). His total personal debt, including the disputed poll tax came to about £12,000.

This type of over-commitment and multiple debt is very difficult to break out of – particularly with the stagnant housing market and the problems of negative equity which prevent trading down as one remedy.

Gopal and his wife had found one answer. They had taken in two students as lodgers to help boost their income. Gopal was 45 and worked as a payroll assistant for a utility company. He earned £790 a month which supported his wife and two children aged seven and six. Three or four years ago he was earning less and interest rates were higher. At this time, his wages were barely enough to cover the cost of the mortgage. Gopal fell behind with the repayments and has been struggling ever since to pay back his arrears. His income had risen recently to £790 a month and interest rates had fallen. He had also taken in two lodgers which provided him with an extra £270 a month. So Gopal arranged to pay a little extra each month – taking his repayments to £590 a month. This still meant that he only had £470 a month left for all his family's needs after paying his mortgage. He still owed £2,000:

> *My salary has gone up and also I take in a couple of tenants.*
> *Therefore it's much easier now than it was three or four years*
> *ago ... All these things are settling down. Therefore, I can now*
> *see a bit more clearly how the money things stand.*

Nick had enormous arrears. Since his wife left three years ago, he had not paid any mortgage and so owed £27,000 in arrears (£750 a month). The house was bought in joint names with his wife and his wife no longer contributed anything. In any case, he believed that the building society has lost the deeds to the house and so could not evict him. He also had a personal overdraft for £15,000 and both gas and electricity arrears. He paid these back when he used fuel as he had prepayment meters for both. Although Nick was earning a relatively high amount (£500 a week), a large proportion went immediately on childminding (£120) and taxi fares (£100). He also gave the childminder £60 a week to buy food for his children. This left him with £220 a week. His mortgage worked out as £173 a week, so even if he was committed to paying it, it would be very difficult to do so.

7   Money management

Not all those in debt are on low incomes. Ten of those interviewed had above-average incomes. One of the main reasons why these people got into debt was poor money management and disorganisation with their finances.

Billy was 45 and earned £22,000 a year as a college lecturer. He also earned about £3,000 a year on ad hoc film projects. Billy had three children, aged 20, 19 and 12. They lived with him one week and his ex-wife the next. Until recently, Billy had also been living with his girlfriend, Sally, but she moved out in November 1991 after a miscarriage. Billy felt that his house was too big for him now:

> I've got a mortgage [£560 a month] I'd rather not have. I would like to have sold it when [Sally] moved out and bought something smaller, but you try and sell a house that you have just bought – people just don't want to know.

Sally's departure had affected Billy's life in many ways:

> I am trying to rationalise all my outgoings because it was easier when [Sally] was here because everything was like planned very well. It was made difficult by the halving of the income – the emotional trauma one goes through as well.

Billy put his children first. He said that his life was:

> Centred around the kids basically. And I'd rather go into debt rather than let them go short.

He realised that he was not very good with managing his money:

> I'm just not a good organiser ... My attitude to money could do with a little attention now and again.

But he had taken action to reflect this:

> I'm not very good with [money], which is why I like to get it on standing orders and then I can forget about it.

Billy paid most of his bills, including his gas bill, by standing order. So why did he get into debt? The main reason was that when Sally left in November 1991, their joint account was stopped and Billy had to open a new account. While he managed to reorganise most bills, he forgot about the gas. Although British Gas sent him bills, Billy did not recognise them:

> *When you are on a standing order, they are statements. And there is no difference between a statement and a bill to look at apart from they say 'disregard it'. I had a whole stack of these which were actually bills which I thought were statements.*

Although Billy noticed that he received red bills, he assumed they were a mistake. He said that he never checked his bank balance or bank statement:

> *It could be that someone has been sharing my account with me and I'd just have no idea.*

Billy was highly committed to his students and his job:

> *I'm a bit of a dreamer as a person anyway. You can look up after working very hard and suddenly two weeks have gone.*

He took only three weeks holiday a year and worked very long hours. Apart from his children and his work, Billy paid little attention to anything – including bills. Billy's gas account was up-to-date when the bank cancelled the standing order late in 1991. Seven months later, he owed £400.

Dan and Jeff were brothers in their early 20s living in what the interviewer described as 'a fluctuating hippy household'. Dan was a trained wood machinist, earning £400 a month for working two days a week. Jeff was a full-time support worker for a health authority, earning £690 a month. Dan supplemented his income, when he could, by playing in a band. When they were booked for a gig, Jeff often acted as the roadie of the band. The income from this was variable, but they could make about £100 a month. Dan and Jeff were both very laid back about money and bills. As Jeff said:

> *I'm not business minded, you know ... I don't really keep a check on my monthly outgoings ... I think I'm getting by. I don't buy a lot. I don't have a car. I feel I live very cheaply.*

Jeff thought he had paid the winter gas bill and so got a shock when the next bill arrived and was for £270 instead of the £130 they had been expecting. It did not worry them, however, and they did not hurry to pay this bill:

> *I don't like rush out and pay them [bills] immediately.*

Jeff summed up their difficulties:

He's [Dan] only poor because he can't find another job. I'm poor because I can't manage money.

Andy simply disliked dealing with paperwork and bills:

I'm just really lazy, because I've got loads of paperwork to do and I just sling it in the corner and just leave it there until it's too late ... It's time more than anything else – being bothered to write the cheque out.

He was a 32 year old publican, earning about £50,000 a year, some of which was ploughed back into this, and other businesses. He received bills for his home, the pub and other properties (about which he would not give much information). He said that he got confused with all the bills and thought he had paid the gas bill for his home. When he received red bills he thought British Gas had made a mistake and just ignored them:

I probably got a disconnection notice or something like that, but I get so many of these things, I just throw them away.

Frank also disliked paying bills. In his words:

It bores me.

He was earning about £25,000 a year as a systems analyst. Although his home and his two children (aged 15 and 20) were in the North, Frank worked in London and commuted at weekends. This disruption often meant he forgot or lost papers. It also made it difficult for him to contact local suppliers personally.

Mohammed and Jenny's income was also above average. Mohammed worked as a chef in a pizza restaurant and earned about £200 a week, depending on overtime. Jenny worked as a computer operator and earned £150 a week. They looked after Jenny's 6 year old daughter. Jenny believed that she and Mohammed were well organised and good at managing their money. But they still struggled to find the money when their quarterly bills came in (and Jenny felt that they always came at once). It was probably the mismatch between the frequency of their weekly income and that of their quarterly bills which caused them problems. But Jenny had a different explanation:

Lack of money. That's it, isn't it, lack of money. I think for a lot of people their salaries are not enough to live on, basically. And I think you need to have a lump sum come from somewhere to get right again ... but the actual salaries for living are not enough.

They were careful not to spend more than they had:

We're as organised as we'll ever be, because I think, 'if you've got it – you've got it.' If you haven't got it, it's not whether you're organised or not.

After having difficulties with the recent batch of quarterly bills, Jenny felt that:

Just now we are starting to balance out. Things are getting up-to-date now.

But Jenny had recently heard that she was being made redundant, and the future looked uncertain.

So far in this chapter we have looked at people on above-average earnings. It is sometimes argued that those on social security or low-paid jobs are not poor because their income is too low, but because they are poor money managers. We have seen in previous chapters that in many instances incomes barely covered outgoings. However carefully people managed their money, there was simply not enough to make ends meet. However, there are poor money managers at all levels of income. While those on higher incomes can often avoid debt even if they are poor managers, those with less money to play with find it more difficult to do so. It must be said, however, that there were very few people on low income who had got into difficulties because of poor money management.

The Khan family should have been receiving about £125 a week extra if they had claimed all the benefits to which they appear entitled. But poor money management contributed to the difficulties they faced. They did not save in advance for bills and there was no regular system for paying. When a bill arrived, they saw what everyone could afford and put it into a kitty and then tried to save to pay the rest. In the case of their recent gas bill, the family were not able to find the money in the time allowed. They also had arrears of £400 poll tax (for which they may be entitled to some rebate) and had run up a £3-4,000 overdraft.

Terry admitted that he would quickly spend any money he had in his hands. He was on Income Support and had direct deductions for rent, water rates, electricity, gas and poll tax. Arrears on all these mounted up because Terry found it very difficult to manage his money. He was pleased to have the responsibility of bill-payment taken out of his hands.

Doug lost his job in September 1991. He accumulated various arrears while in work, as a result of his drinking and gambling habits. Doug said that he disliked debt, but his dislike was not strong enough to affect his spending behaviour and money management.

Many of those on low incomes actually managed their money surprisingly well. Norman admitted that he was not a naturally good manager but had learnt, through necessity, to cope on a low income. He had always found it difficult to manage money and relied first on his wife and then his mother to sort out bills. Now, on Income Support of £84 a fortnight, he was having to manage everything on his own. He paid most things weekly, but still received quarterly electricity and telephone bills. He did have gas arrears, but was now paying these off through his token meter. He had no other arrears.

Ron was an eligible non-claimant of Family Credit, earning £450 a month with two children. Despite the fact that he was entitled to about £35 a week on top of his earnings and £75 a month Child Benefit, he was one of the six people interviewed who had not got into arrears. His success was partly due to very careful money management. This skill was developed with the help of Ron's former employer who was an accountant. She gave him much advice on budgeting and advised Ron to go on a gas prepayment plan to avoid quarterly bills. Ron was terrified of large bills, threatening letters and debt and so kept close control of his income and outgoings. His rent and water rates of £23 a week were his first priority. He then ensured that there was enough money to cover his monthly bills – gas £40 a month, electricity £90 a month and poll tax £44 a month. These bills added up to £274 a month, leaving Ron and the family with £251 a month, or £58 a week, for all other outgoings, such as food, clothes and transport. Despite this, he had no arrears.

8   Absence from home

One of the other main explanations for debt among those on higher than average incomes is absence from home for long periods of time. Some people do not take measures to ensure that their bills get paid. Because of their absence from home, these people are often likely to be unresponsive to any contact sent to them to try and recover the debt. In addition to the five people whose circumstances are described below, another ten could not be contacted by PSI interviewers because they were away from home for an extended period. In one instance a man was away working on the North Sea Oil rigs; another person was a singer and away on a tour of Europe.

On business

Eddy's working practices caused him to get into debt. He was a sales representative, earning about £22,000 a year. His job often took him away from home – sometimes abroad:

> *I was cut off last year and it wasn't because of lack of funds. It was because I'm away a lot, I travel a lot. Sometimes I'm not here for a long time and my post is only attended by myself … It was my fault for not paying the bill, so you can't blame anyone except myself.*

Eddy received quarterly gas, electricity and telephone bills. He paid his water rates annually. This method of payment did not cause financial problems for Eddy, but it did cause administrative problems. He was aware of this, but had always had quarterly bills:

> *That's the way that I've done it ever since I – this is the second home I've had – ever since I started to have my own place, which must be the last 12 years. I've always done it that way. I would actually like to do direct debit. It's just a matter of getting round to it.*

Fraser's absence from home did not cause him to get behind with his bill, but it did cause difficulties in communications with British Gas. Fraser was a 43 year old freelance consultant who lived in a large, modern, detached house in an affluent village in the Home Counties. He had recently been working in the North on a major contract and earned about £40,000 a year. Fraser's absence from home did not cause him to get into debt, as he had all his post redirected by a neighbour who looked after his house while he was away.

Fraser's difficulties, however, concerned disputes over the estimated bills that British Gas sent him. As he was not at home he could not check the meter at the time and although he suspected that the estimates were inaccurate, he found it difficult to contact British Gas North Thames while he was busy working in Lancashire. He did get in touch on several occasions, but eventually decided to leave things until he returned back home.

In Frank's case it was weekly commuting that caused problems. He worked in London during the week, returning to his home in the North-East at the weekend. He therefore saw his post once a week. Frank's commuting and his attitude to bill-paying ('it bores me') combined at the end of 1991, so that he 'just left a quarter' – that is, he just did not pay his bill for that quarter. In the winter of 1992, Frank received a bill for two quarters and this came to about £750. He felt that this was too high and asked British Gas to check the meter. They said they would do that, but it would cost £30. Frank 'was a bit cheesed about that' and did not bother having it checked.

Frank said that he 'had other things on my mind' at the time, although he did not specify what they were. He remembered receiving bills and letters, but did not take much notice of them. Eventually he was disconnected.

Family reasons

Margaret moved into her present unfurnished flat nine months ago but she had only lived in the flat for a total of two months; the rest of the time she had been in Scotland due to the serious health problems in her family. Margaret was a bit confused about the details of what had happened in the last nine months and generally felt that things were getting on top of her. During the interview, Margaret seemed to be a 'sad and anxious' woman who worried greatly about things, according to the interviewer. Margaret did remember that she gave a friend some money to keep up her £50 a month gas payments. She was therefore shocked to find that when she came back from Scotland, British Gas said that she owed £500.

Rosa went to South America every year for two or three months over the summer to visit her family. During this time, her cousin lived in the flat. Rosa's ability to speak English was not very good and she was vague about the exact arrangements she had with her cousin. She was also vague about whether she had even been disconnected at all. Her quarterly winter bill was £60 which she said she paid in full and her next bill was about £50. She thought she may have received a disconnection letter, but then had difficulty remembering anything else. It seems that she went to South America without paying her bill and then was disconnected while she was away.

In hospital

Audrey was 52 and suffered from rheumatism and asthma. She was waiting for a hip replacement operation. Three years ago Audrey went into hospital for three weeks, but was disconnected soon after she came out. Audrey was not sure exactly why she got behind with her gas payments. She had been paying fortnightly with a payment book, but because of her disability was unable to go to the showroom herself and relied on family and neighbours to pay. She thought she missed a couple of payments and that while she was in hospital she may have missed another one or two.

An alternative explanation could lie in the fact that Audrey's daughter had asked the Department of Social Security and British Gas, on Audrey's request, if Audrey could have her gas paid through direct deductions from her social security benefit (Fuel Direct). Both organisations said that she would have to be in arrears first and so, perhaps, Audrey's daughter allowed her to miss payments so that she would get into arrears and go on Fuel Direct, which is actually what happened. Audrey had been on the scheme for three years and she had actually received a rebate of £140 from British Gas due to over-payment.

Non-resident landlord

Amit was a busy man. He had a full-time job, ran two businesses and rented out a house to three (sometimes four) couples. He did not live at the house even though his name was still on all the bills. The tenants' rent included all bills and every now and then (usually about once a month) Amit dropped in to the house to pick up his mail. Sometimes he was very busy and did not come in for a while.

The interview was carried out with Isobel who was the oldest woman in the house and knew most about the running of the household. Isobel and others in the house noticed that the March gas bill along with other post had not been collected. They put this down to the landlord's busy lifestyle:

> *He works a lot of shifts. He works afternoons and nights and things like that. He's sort of running around like a headless chicken a lot of the time.*

They then noticed that the red bill and other letters arrived from British Gas. Again, they left them for Amit to collect, which he failed to do. Amit was usually very efficient in taking care of the bills and was a very good landlord. Isobel felt that he should not take all the blame:

> *I suppose in a way it's our fault as well as his, because we are not very communicative with him. We don't ring him up and say, 'the electric bill's here.' We wait for him to come.*

But British Gas arrived before Amit:

> *They arrived at the door. They said, 'We've come to cut the gas off', and she [one of the other tenants] said, 'It's nowt to do with us, you've got to see the landlady'. They said, 'We've got a right to cut it off and you've had notification and everything'.*

Isobel and her fellow tenants felt that:

> *Because we are not owners of the property there is nothing we could do.*

9   Difficulties with payment methods

We have already seen that absence from home can lead to fuel debt and even disconnection for those who receive quarterly bills. Direct debit or standing order payments could easily overcome these problems. For Eddy, quarterly bills were inappropriate because he was often working away from home and did not have his mail redirected. He said that he had always used this method, but would consider a direct debit arrangement now that he had been disconnected. Dan and Jeff were very disorganised as were Amit and his tenants. They too could have avoided getting into arrears by setting up a direct debit arrangement.

Quarterly bills

Quarterly bills (and twice yearly bills – as in the case of water rates) are especially problematic for people living on low, weekly incomes.

Maxine was in her early 20s and looked after her one year old baby with Income Support and Child Benefit of £71.05 a week. She received quarterly gas and electric bills and, when she received her last gas bill, had to negotiate an arrangement giving her time to pay.

Mohammed and Jenny also had difficulties paying their winter quarterly bill. For the last four years, this bill had been £80. This year it was £190. They had managed to pay £120 when they received their next quarterly bill which was for £200. This was also much higher than they expected. They disputed the bill, but British Gas would not accept this and so Jenny arranged to pay it back in instalments. This was a very informal agreement. Jenny just said she would pay what she could when she could. Jenny paid some money (she was not sure exactly how much), but they were eventually given a deadline by which time they had to pay the whole bill. They did not manage to do so and were disconnected. They then managed to borrow some money to cover the arrears, but when they went to pay this at the showroom, they were told that they had to pay for all the gas they had consumed to date before they could be reconnected.

Mohammed and Jenny were furious that, as they saw it, they had to pay a bill they had not even seen. They could not afford to pay it and so were left without gas for three weeks while they tried to raise the money (a total of £300).

Sunil and the Khan family also received quarterly bills even though these households received their income on a weekly basis. The Khan household were not able to find enough money to pay this bill in the time given. If they received weekly or monthly bills the difficulties may be reduced.

Some people recognised that quarterly bills were difficult to pay and realised that there were alternative ways of paying, such as payment plans. But payment plans sometimes caused problems too.

Payment plans

Lisa and Mark had not been disconnected but had experienced difficulties with their payment plan when they were paying £34 a month by standing order (this included an amount for arrears). When she got married, Lisa changed her surname and the bank cancelled their standing orders without informing her. After six weeks, British Gas wrote to say that they were being taken off the payment scheme as they had received no money from the bank. Lisa rang the bank and discovered what had happened. Lisa was angry with the bank for not informing her that the standing order was cancelled, but she was also angry that British Gas had not informed her sooner that they had not received their payment. When she rang British Gas to complain, they said:

> *It's not policy, we don't do that. It's your responsibility for making sure it's done.*

Billy had a similar problem when his standing order was cancelled by the bank.

Malcolm was paying £6 or £7 a week on a gas prepayment plan and was keeping up his payments despite the fact that he was on Income Support. Problems arose, however, when he ran out of slips in his payment book. He asked for a new one in person and by phone. It did not arrive, so Malcolm still paid his instalments in person and got some kind of receipt for them. Despite the fact that he showed them his receipts, British Gas subsequently said they had no record of his payments. At the same time as this happened, Malcolm received a winter bill for £500 which was unusually high because he had had a gas leak. Malcolm was upset that British Gas did not believe him:

> *I had a stand up argument with the Gas Board and, I felt a bit of a pratt as I felt as though I was telling lies. I felt as though I was being put on the spot ... I've had that many arguments*

with the Gas Board over this. You see, me, meself, I've never had gas arrears. I've been a tenant for 15 years or more and never had gas arrears. But all of a sudden, I owe all this phenomenal amount and I don't know where it's coming from. I very rarely have the heating on.

Malcolm was now paying £14 a week through Fuel Direct.

10   Unexpectedly high bills

Most people said that the bills they received were roughly what they expected and that the difficulties they had in paying were due to other factors such as low income. As Viv says:

> It was not unusually high, it was just the circumstances. I just wasn't getting any money, full stop, from my husband.

But some people did feel that their bill was much higher than usual and a number thought that there had been a mistake. For the last four years, Mohammed's winter bill had worked out at about £80. In March 1992, the bill came to £190. He could see no reason why the bill should be any greater this time as both he and his wife were still out at work most of the day and that winter had been rather mild. According to Mohammed, British Gas refused to check the meter and so Mohammed and his wife arranged a repayment plan.

Frank had asked for his (higher than average) bill to be checked and British Gas agreed, providing he pay £30. He was not very happy about that.

Clive and Barbara were staggered to receive a quarterly bill in the spring of 1992 for £160 when their previous bill at this time was £110. Again they had expected a lower bill because of the mildness of winter.

Maxine moved into her small council flat in November 1991 and since then had received what she considered to be high bills. She disputed all her bills, wondering if British Gas were trying to make her pay for an ex-tenant. When her meter was changed in the summer of 1992, her subsequent bills were much lower even though she was using similar amounts of gas.

Len and Gopal, along with some others in the sample, said that they had received higher bills because of the increase in gas prices, not because they had used more gas. As Gopal said:

> Before privatisation, the price of gas or electricity was much lower.

The issue of estimated bills cropped up repeatedly in the sample. Fraser moved into his home in 1988 and since then had received very high estimated bills. He worked away from home for long periods and so probably did not use as much gas as the previous occupiers and could not check an estimated bill soon after he received one. He eventually took a reading which showed that he had been paying much more than he should do. He wrote three or four letters to British Gas saying that he would not pay any more money until they checked his meter for themselves. He wanted British Gas to tell him when they would be able to visit so that he could ensure he would be home but he could only make weekends or evenings. He said that British Gas refused to do this. He had already paid £700 over a year and refused to pay the £500 which British Gas said he owed.

Fraser also pointed out that British Gas bills were contradictory; on one original bill he was charged £500 and on the red bill which followed, he was charged £300 (despite the fact that he had not paid anything in between). Whatever the facts of the dispute (and we only have Fraser's version), Fraser decided to stop paying his bills in protest at the way the dispute was being handled. He has now been disconnected. Fraser probably accrued arrears when he stopped paying for his gas. He had kept all documentation referring to this dispute and was quite happy to go to court in order to get compensation from British Gas.

Just before the interviewing began in July 1992, the 1986 Gas Act was amended so that a gas supplier now will not be entitled to disconnect a gas supply for any amount which is 'genuinely in dispute'. It is unclear who decides whether a bill is genuinely in dispute and how they do so, but this may prevent some unnecessary disconnections.

11   British Gas mistakes?

Dave was convinced that he was disconnected by complete mistake. He was 43 and worked as a painter/decorator, earning about £16,000 a year. His wife, Silvana, was 26. She worked part-time with her mother in the family's second-hand business. She earned about £2,600 a year. They had a three year old child. Dave and Silvana received quarterly bills. They had always paid this way:

> Except when we couldn't pay it, and then we made an arrangement to pay it.

This was some time ago, when they had a large winter bill. They paid it off in instalments, and had paid all arrears by the time the next quarter's bill arrived. But this year they were disconnected.

In the summer of 1992, they received a quarterly bill for about £50, which was not unusually high and was not difficult for them to pay. As always, they put the bill aside to wait for the red to arrive and then pay that bill. Ten days after they received the original bill, they were disconnected. They had received no other communications. When Dave and Silvana contacted British Gas:

> They told us that they had been informed the house was occupied by squatters, and they'd been told to take the meter out.

It was certainly true that there were squatters living in the house next door and so there could have been a mistake about the number of the house. But Dave and Silvana feel that it was obvious which house had squatters as the house next door was boarded up, while theirs looked just like an average house. Although Dave and Silvana protested that they were not squatters, British Gas would not admit to having made a mistake. Only one person they spoke to came anywhere near to admitting a mistake:

> One man we spoke to said, 'Yes, well we have been known to make mistakes; I'm not saying we are in this case, but we have

> *been known to. All I can do is to apologise and arrange to have it reconnected immediately.'*

But to add insult to injury, British Gas then told Dave and Silvana that they would not be reconnected until they paid the £50 bill that they had received ten days before.

Dave and Silvana paid the bill and were reconnected three days after their disconnection. The experience left them bitter. They were a very security conscious family, having been burgled three times to date. Their experience with British Gas reinforced their fears. The front door was already festooned with locks and there were bars on the back windows. Since the disconnection, Dave had installed a security camera over the front door. This now faced into the room.

In this case, as in all the other cases in this study, we do not have the British Gas explanation of what happened. It is possible that Dave and Silvana were not telling the whole truth or leaving out certain facts about what happened – but our interviewer feels that they were being honest. It could be that they are telling the whole truth, but that British Gas may have their side to the story.

12 Working the system?

It is every company's nightmare that people are using their services and taking advantage of their credit facilities without feeling any responsibility to pay. Even worse than this, is the idea that people are deliberately 'working the system'. That is, they deliberately use services without any real intention of paying and then, with their knowledge of the supplier's debt recovery procedures, make up excuses and repay some money in dribs and drabs to keep the supplier from taking serious action. This fear has increased in recent years in part as a result of the high levels of deliberate non-payment of the poll tax.

It must be said, however, that there is very little evidence of people deliberately working the system in this study. Most people felt a very strong responsibility to pay for the gas they used and to keep out of debt. For those without such a moral sense, disconnection and subsequent court action was a deterrent against getting into debt. An earlier study of fuel debts concluded:

> As with every effective deterrent, those whose activities are open to influence are not those who suffer the sanction. Thus if an employer were to employ draconian penalties to those who claimed sickness in order to deter malingerers, the malingerers would come to work and the genuinely sick would suffer the penalties ... So, with disconnection: those who can pay get the message, while those who cannot suffer loss of supplies (Berthoud 1981).

So those who can afford to pay generally will pay. Of course they may leave it to the last minute and get into arrears, but it is unlikely that many so-called 'won't pays' will allow themselves to be disconnected. It must be said, however, that about about one in eight of the customers whom we tried to contact had permanently moved out of their homes, according to information from neighbours and other sources. These people may have moved away in order to avoid paying their arrears. But according to British Gas records, some of these had been in touch after disconnection and so the 'moonlight flit' theory should not be accepted without question.

The closest example of someone working the system was Nick. Nick was fairly wealthy for a lone parent, earning £500 a week. But he had got into debt because he was overcommitted financially, disorganised and felt little responsibility to pay his suppliers or creditors. He was a man who was determined not to let anything affect his preferred lifestyle. He kept his job even though it necessitated high expenditure on childminding and taxi fares. He also felt that it was important for him to socialise after work for an hour or two:

> *I don't drink that heavily, just beer. I play hard in that I have a high pressured job and I socialise for a couple of hours after work before I collect the kids. That is my social life. I'm with the kids ever since ... I've had them all the time and that means every weekend.*

Nick admitted that:

> *I have a very bad attitude to money. It just goes through my fingers ... I'm totally useless, unbelievably useless.*

Although Nick had an income which was above average, it was barely enough to cover his outgoings on his mortgage repayments, childcare costs and taxi fares to and from the childminder and work. Over-commitment was not a full explanation for his problems, however, as Nick felt a lack of responsibility to deal with his financial situation. He owed £27,000 in mortgage arrears, as well as £15,000 to the bank and gas and electricity arrears. He had also paid no poll tax or water rates, but he did not know exactly how much he owed:

> *It's not that I choose not to pay. I just haven't bothered – not even considered it ... I don't worry too much about things these days. The amount of money they are going to be coming for eventually, there's no way they are going to get it.*

Nick was so deep in debt he had stopped trying to avoid it, if he had ever made much attempt to do so in the first place. He did feel that:

> *Things might change when I move out of this place. When I further resume a proper mortgage position or even a rental position.*

Nick's attitude to money has been mentioned earlier ('Me and money just don't mix'). He was rather dilatory with bill-paying:

> *I ignore them ... I leave them to the last minute, which is a habit I've got into ... I don't like paying bills.*

But Nick was not just lazy. He was rather more calculating than that:

I did actually go and arrange a [gas] Budget Scheme ... Really that was just a sort of holding them up process because I had them going for about another eight months.

Nick deliberately waited until the last minute and then contacted British Gas to try and win more time. He almost avoided disconnection as he had intended to get in touch with British Gas just before, but mistimed it:

When I knew they were one hundred per cent serious that they were going to cut me off on a particular date, I intended to contact them and then forgot. If I had just rung them and said, 'OK, look, I want a key meter instead of disconnection,' I would have got a key meter ... I know I could have had that by contacting them by phone. I just forgot. I was playing it to the last minute and then forgot on the vital day. It just slipped my mind and it cost me £64 [reconnection charge].

Nick did not even feel that he would have to pay up eventually:

Because at the end of the day, when it got to figures of £900 or £1,000 and I was also not sure if I would be on the premises for the next three months ... I don't know if I'll be here three months from now, so there was no point in my paying a £900 bill ... there are ways of being unlocatable.

Nick did not manage to escape from British Gas and was disconnected. After reconnection, he had a prepayment meter installed and was paying his arrears as he used gas. Nick certainly felt no obligation to pay for his gas, but this attitude was perhaps less of a barrier to payment than the facts of his financial situation. These facts put the importance of his attitude into some perspective.

There was also some evidence that other people deliberately delayed paying their bills. Many said that they waited for the red bill before paying. This was sometimes because they needed time to save up the money, sometimes because it was simply a habit and sometimes because they wanted to keep money in their bank rather than go to someone else's. It was felt to be quite acceptable to pay after receiving the red bill. They did not feel that they were getting into debt by doing so.

In Andy's case he delayed paying his gas bill, and clearly mistimed things. Andy, himself, said that his non-payment was simply a mistake. He usually paid his bill when he received a red bill and thought he had done so in this case. He did not read any subsequent mail from British Gas because he thought it was either a mistake or junk mail. However, he also said that an engineer came round once to disconnect his electricity supply which does not support his statement that he always paid his bills when he receives a reminder. He also had a very good idea of the debt recovery policies of the utilities. He knew roughly how long it would take for British Gas to disconnect after an original bill and he said that he always paid British Telecom quickly because they disconnect very quickly. It is possible, therefore, that rather than being disorganised, Andy deliberately delayed payments for as long as he thought he could. In the case of electricity, he misjudged this and someone came to disconnect him (although he paid them when they visited and so avoided disconnection). In the case of gas, he misjudged again and was not in when he was disconnected. Once again, he had the money to pay his bill immediately afterwards.

Other than Nick, and perhaps Andy, there is no hint of people working the system. In fact, quite the reverse. People were committed to paying debts and generally did not deliberately delay payment beyond a red bill. In most cases, people on very low incomes felt a strong responsibility to repay their debts. Ray said:

> *They are providing a service; you've got to pay for it. If you don't pay, you don't get the service. Common sense.*

Gary believed in paying his bills, but put the gas bill below the mortgage in his list of priorities:

> *I'm not in the habit – if I can pay me bill, I pay it, you know? I don't ... try to skank anybody or anything like that. But I'd got the mortgage and everything, and things got a bit tight, and I just couldn't pay the bill. Simple as that.*

Although Gary believed in paying his bills, he was certainly not happy about British Gas:

> *In the winter months, especially just after Christmas, you just get hammered by a big bill, and it's just a nightmare. Quite hon – I really think – my own opinion is that the Gas Board are just atrocious – the way the prices are charged. With the amount of profit they make, it's just ridiculous really. But you can't go anywhere else, can you? It's like gas or electricity, and they're both as bad as each other.*

The three issues of prices, profits and monopoly were mentioned by many people in the sample. But the commitment to pay was so strong that dissatisfaction with these aspects of British Gas did not seem to weaken it. Gary felt, however, that British Gas (or 'The Gas Board') as he and many others continued to call it, was much better than British Telecom:

> *I mean in all honesty I've not got a gripe with the Gas Board ... I just think the way they charge and the profit they make is ridiculous. But ... it doesn't grieve me that you pay whatever, £40, for reconnection charge because you actually see the guy come out and he's actually, physically working, putting the meter. And you can understand that that's gonna cost money. I mean ... like the telephone, if you get cut off, like at the press of a button, you're back on – you pay! That annoys me. But with the Gas, I mean in all honesty, the Gas has been – out of all the – the sort of privatised industries, the Gas are not too bad, really... there's enough stuff comes through the door to try and help you. But if you haven't got the money, it's not gonna help anyway ... It's not like the telephone – three weeks, you're [cut] off if you haven't paid.*

Clive and Barbara had a strong sense of responsibility to pay their bills and had not got into arrears with their gas. But they realised that other people were less able to pay their way:

> *I'm a great believer that people should pay their own way in life and if they don't, they deserve the consequences. Now there are some people who can't pay ... Some pensioners do not. All they have is what they get from the Post Office every Thursday morning and that doesn't go a long way. So for those people, I do sympathise. I think that on those occasions, there should be some system to make sure that they do not go without the basic needs which are heating and food ... And even having said all that, I don't think it's the Gas Board, the gas companies, that should have to foot the bill. Society has to foot the bill.*

There is, then, little evidence of 'won't pays' who have been disconnected; on the contrary people who had been disconnected frequently blamed no-one but themselves and felt a strong obligation to pay all that they owed. Gary echoed the conclusions of the 1981 study of fuel debt about the purpose of disconnection:

> *Well, obviously, it's a punishment, in't it? It's a punishment for your bad behaviour. I suppose, obviously, if they didn't disconnect, there's people who would just take the mickey ...*

> *there's people who just don't want to pay ... no matter what British Gas did, if you halved the prices tomorrow there'd still be people who didn't wanna pay it really.*

This is a poignant remark given the evidence that three-quarters of the people who had been disconnected lived on social security payments or low wages. It merely highlights the paradox whereby those at whom the deterrent is aimed are not those who suffer the sanction.

Part II
DEBT RECOVERY PROCEDURES
AND DISCONNECTION

13   British Gas procedures for helping people in arrears

British Gas procedures for helping people in arrears avoid disconnection are laid down in a number of documents. Condition 12A of the *Authorisation to British Gas* states that customers should not be cut off from their gas supply if they agree and keep to a payment arrangement to repay their arrears at a rate they can afford. Even if they are not able to maintain such an arrangement, disconnection should still be avoided by offering them a prepayment meter. A prepayment meter will only be refused if it is unsafe or impractical to install one. In their summary document, *British Gas, Principles for the collection of domestic gas debt*, revised June 1990, British Gas make a commitment that:

> Disconnection of a gas supply will only take place as a last resort, when every other alternative has been exhausted ... The Company's policy is to encourage customers in difficulties to get in touch as early as possible so that advice and assistance can be given. Customers who make contact and indicate that they have a debt problem will be routed to the appropriate staff. British Gas will ensure that customers with payment difficulties who make contact with appropriate staff will receive sympathetic treatment at all times ... In cases where the customer fails to make contact with debt collection staff, the latter will deliver a *Helpline Pack* including a copy of the Code of Practice and a customer Helpline card. This card encourages the customer to contact the Company with a specific payment offer and/or contact either the Department of Social Security or an appropriate advice agency. It also gives the customer the option of seeking a prepayment meter.

So why is it that these procedures did not prevent disconnection in 15,707 cases in 1992? The explanation given by British Gas is that customers simply do not get in touch with them. According to their figures, there was no contact with customers in 62 per cent of disconnection cases for the quarter ending December 1992. In the majority of the remaining cases (34 per cent), customers made payment plans but did not keep them up and broke contact with British Gas (see Appendix 3). It is important to investigate the issue of non-contact as it is seen as a major problem by many utility companies, along with creditors in other fields.

Demystifying non-contact

A recent study of electricity customers found that the level of contact reported by customers was greater than that recorded by the electricity companies (SCPR, 1983). Our research with gas customers finds a similar difference. While some of the discrepancy could be explained by customers over-stating the amount of contact they had with British Gas, we are confident about the honesty of all but one or two of the people interviewed. In some cases, customers provided copies of letters sent to British Gas as evidence of contact. In others, they provided lengthy and detailed accounts of correspondence, phone calls and visits. We conclude, therefore, that British Gas statistics on non-contact do not accurately reflect the amount of contact taking place. This spans all forms from letters written to British Gas, to telephone calls, to personal visits to the showroom.

Interviews were conducted with 11 people who were categorised by British Gas as 'broken contact' cases. By British Gas' definition, these are people who have set up payment plans, broken them and then broken off contact with British Gas. All 11 of those interviewed in this category admitted that they had had a payment plan and then been disconnected (although two of these were rather vague about the details). So, in a very narrow sense, it may seem that these people fit into this category. Some people, however, were still trying to pay something and were telling British Gas that they were trying to pay fairly soon before disconnection.

In the 'broken contact' category, Sid had been in touch with British Gas on numerous occasions. As well as personal visits and telephone calls, he had written three letters to the company explaining his situation. Percy was having difficulties with his payment plan and both went to the showroom and telephoned British Gas offering £20 to avoid disconnection. Len got in touch when he received the Helpline Card, but heard nothing in reply and was disconnected soon afterwards.

The use of the title 'broken contact' implies that customers deliberately stop paying their bills and do not get in touch again until after disconnection. Although there are undoubtedly some customers for whom this is the case, the term is misleading since there are also some who do keep in touch and offer some payment before disconnection.

A second group comprised people on payment plans who had not been disconnected. Seven of the 12 interviewed in this category were on prepayment plans and five were on repayment plans. None of these had been disconnected, so everyone fitted the category.

The third group covered people who, according British Gas, had not been in touch before disconnection, but *had* been in touch within two weeks after. Seven of the 12 interviewed in this category had not been in touch with British Gas before disconnection and so were classified correctly. The remaining five, however, had all been in touch *before* disconnection and so were classified incorrectly by British Gas.

Terry, for example, had been in touch a number of times to get onto Fuel Direct. Malcolm had both written and also asked personally for a new payment book so that he could keep up his instalments. Mike had phoned the Staines office after receiving the disconnection letter to discuss his difficulties, but then engineers from his local office said they knew nothing about this when they disconnected him. Tariq had telephoned British Gas after receiving the reminder letter and then the disconnection letter and Ben telephoned British Gas after receiving the Helpline Pack (he does not remeber receiving any other communication). Ben explained that he was having difficulties and also sent off a form to apply for Fuel Direct. He was disconnected the following week and he went on Fuel Direct afterwards.

The greatest discrepancy, however, was in the fourth group – people recorded by British Gas as not having been in touch either *before* disconnection, or within two weeks *after* disconnection. Only three of the ten people interviewed fitted the criteria. Of course part of the explanation for this may lie in the fact that this group would include people who had moved away and that we, too, would find it difficult to make contact. There was certainly some evidence that this was true. In addition to the ten people interviewed there were another seven who had, in fact, moved from the address.

Of the seven who do not fit the criteria, three had been in touch before disconnection, but *not* soon afterwards. Fraser had a great deal of contact with British Gas over the estimated bills which he disputes. He wrote three or four letters, but only received standard replies with no mention of the points he made. He telephoned British Gas, but was told to 'put it in writing'. He did so, but 'they just ignore you'.

Ibrahim had lots of contact with British Gas before disconnection:

> *I phoned them anytime I received any letter ... Since I couldn't pay I naturally let them know my condition and told them everything. But to my surprise, they just came in and nobody opened the door for them, but they forced it open.*

Ibrahim did not think it was worth getting in touch after disconnection.

Two people had not been in touch before disconnection, but *did* get in touch soon after. Frank telephoned soon after he was disconnected, but was not able to arrange repayment and reconnection until some time later. Wendy went to see British Gas a couple of days after disconnection to ask for a prepayment meter which was installed about four days later.

Another two had been in touch both before *and* soon after disconnection. Billy rang British Gas when he received the Warrant Notice and explained that his standing order had been cancelled by the bank. He asked for two more weeks to get to the showroom and pay the bill. British Gas agreed to this, but then he received another letter. He rang again and this time he was told to pay immediately. Billy explained that he had been told he could have some more time to pay, but:

> *They say that they had no record of that. That's the trouble with using the phone – it's not recorded.*

Billy was reconnected soon after disconnection.

It is clear that the statistics quoted earlier fail to reflect what is going on at the local level. It is equally clear that the category 'broken contact' is misleading. We can therefore conclude that non-contact and broken contact only provide part of the explanation for why people are disconnected. In order to understand more fully the reasons for disconnection, it is necessary to assess the procedures and policies British Gas use to help people pay their arrears and so avoid disconnection. Although the best method to help someone in difficulties depends on their circumstances, British Gas generally prefers to put someone on a payment plan first of all. If this fails, there is then the safety net of a prepayment meter, or in some cases, Fuel Direct. These strategies for avoiding disconnection are examined in the next two chapters.

14   Payment plans

Payment plans are designed to make it easier for customers to pay for their gas. For the purposes of this study, we distinguish between two types of payment plans. *Repayment* plans are set up when someone has already got into arrears, for example, with a quarterly bill. They cannot afford to pay the bill in one go, so arrange with British Gas to pay their arrears in instalments. The rules governing how much is paid back and over what period are open to negotiation between the customer and local staff. *Prepayment* plans are sometimes called 'budget schemes'. These allow customers to spread the cost of their annual gas bill in equal instalments throughout the year. Customers are usually given the option of weekly, fortnightly or monthly payment methods. Flexible prepayment schemes allow customers to pay whatever they can, when they can, towards their next quarterly bill. If any money is outstanding when the bill is issued, this has to be settled in the standard timing.

The distinction between repayment and prepayment plans is not wholly clear. For example, someone who gets into arrears may wish to pay them off by negotiating a repayment plan. At the same time, they may feel it is wise to set up a weekly prepayment plan to avoid building up arrears in the future. It could also be the case that someone on a prepayment plan falls behind with their instalments and eventually has to negotiate repaying their arrears on top of their regular prepayments. Despite this overlap, the distinction is a useful one, as a repayment plan indicates that someone has recently been in arrears, while a prepayment plan is not necessarily such an indicator.

Twelve families were on payment plans and had not been disconnected. Six of these had not been disconnected because they had not been in arrears. All of these were on prepayment plans and tended to have higher incomes than others in the survey. The remaining six who *had* all been in arrears had at some stage been on a repayment plan and avoided disconnection.

Successful repayment plans
Although relatively high income is part of the explanation of why people on payment plans avoid debt and disconnection, those with repayment plans

were not on high incomes. Mavis had recently been made unemployed and was not claiming the Unemployment Benefit to which she was probably entitled. She was therefore living on her husband Pete's income of £100, from which they were paying £40 a week rent. Even if Mavis was not entitled to Unemployment Benefit, the couple should still have received Housing Benefit to help pay their rent. At the time of the interview they were left with only £60 a week, which was less than a couple on Income Support would receive.

Toni and Maxine were both lone mothers receiving only Child Benefit, One Parent Benefit and Income Support. Brenda received only £55 a week from her state pension. Hannah's situation was a difficult one for the benefit system to cope with. Her 18 year old daughter was still at school and Hannah worked as a freelance artist. Hannah's sources of income were rather unusual. Her rent was paid by her ex-husband. She had a lodger who gave her £60 a week and she sold some of her paintings when she could. It is difficult to know what Hannah was entitled to receive from the social security system, but it is clear that she was on a low income.

Lisa and Mark had had arrears on their gas bills in the past. After getting married six months ago, they moved into their new home – a small, modern, terraced house. They had been in arrears with their gas in their previous flat and had set up a repayment plan to pay these back. At this time, they were on very low incomes. Lisa was earning £5,400 a year and Mark £6,000 and they were receiving quarterly bills. Since then they have managed to pay their arrears off.

High income is therefore not an adequate explanation for why some people in arrears avoid disconnection. Part of the answer lies in people's attitudes. Despite the difficulties of living on Income Support, Maxine was anxious to avoid disconnection:

> *I never actually try and make it reach that stage. I'd just have a nervous breakdown if it reached that stage.*

But she was not surprised that other people in her position were less successful:

> *I've seen a lot of people on IS and they just can't manage. They just fall behind with the bills and stress ... I said to myself, the most important thing is the first thing when my bill comes is to get it paid as quickly as possible.*

Maxine received quarterly bills and then negotiated repayments if she could not afford to pay the whole bill off in one go.

Brenda said that her main priority with her money was:

To pay them [gas and electricity] bills, yes. I know they're the most important and if I let them go too much I ain't going to be able to catch up with them, and that is my main worry, that they're cut off.

Hannah felt that she was managing:

By the skin of my teeth, by juggling.

She was keen to avoid disconnection for psychological reasons:

You need your hot water and things just to keep up your morale.

Of the six families who had arrears which they repaid through a repayment plan, only one, Lisa and Mark, were now on a *prepayment* plan. After they paid off their arrears, Lisa's mother advised them to go on a weekly prepayment plan to avoid future debt and they did so. When they got married, however, Lisa changed her surname and the standing order arrangement was automatically cancelled. The bank did not inform them and British Gas only told her after two monthly payments had been missed. It was difficult for Lisa and Mark to repay these new arrears but by now their joint income had increased to £17,900 a year and so they managed to find the money and avoid disconnection.

The others all received quarterly bills and negotiated repayment arrangements when necessary. So far they had avoided disconnection, but for how much longer? The 'success' of these payment arrangements is therefore debatable. If we visited these people in a year's time, it is possible that some of them may have been disconnected. It could be argued that these customers should set up prepayment plans instead of continuing to receive quarterly bills and struggle to repay them. They have not set up prepayment plans for various reasons, such as low awareness, dislike of prepayment plans and difficulties in negotiating an acceptable level of repayments.

Brenda was not aware that her payments could be spread throughout the year. She would actually like to pay in this way, but had not thought to enquire about the possibility. Hannah was aware of prepayment plans, but had had difficulties negotiating a payment rate which British Gas would accept. Maxine felt that a more permanent weekly payment plan would be a good idea if the payments were set at a reasonable rate. She was once given an amount to pay per week which she felt was too high and so continued to receive quarterly bills.

Since Maxine moved into her current flat in November 1991, she had received high quarterly bills. Although she had queried some of them, she always managed to pay them. In the summer of 1992, she received a bill for £270. She knew she would be unable to pay this off in one lump sum but wished to clear it as soon as possible so got in touch with British Gas:

> *I told them over the phone. I just told them that there was no way I could pay for it all at once. I said I wanted to get it out of the way and over and done with. That's why I said to them I wanted to pay it off high as, you know what I mean, just get it out of the way. That's why I paid so much, because I know most people just pay only £20, you know, £10, but I didn't want that. I just wanted to get it right out of my head.*

It wasn't easy to find the money:

> *I starved myself. Made sure my daughter was all right and saved up the money in the Post Office until I could pay it. I paid £70 one week, then I paid £50, then another £60 ... I made sure I had £10 for shopping or whatever, so I was really drawing the line thin. So she was on tinned food and I was on whatever scraps were left over.*

After this, Maxine thought it best to go on a prepayment plan:

> *It's supposed to be better for you – what a load of crap! They sent me this book and they wanted me to pay £54 a month for gas in here ... I couldn't believe, I said, 'I'm on Income Support, I'm a single parent, I've got no gas cooker'.*

They told her not to worry because she would get a rebate for overpayments:

> *But you don't get it back. They just put it onto another bill.*

Although Maxine had avoided disconnection so far, she did have difficulty finding the money for bills:

> *It's really stressful. Specially when you're on IS. You don't get that much money.*

Maxine was convinced that her high bills were the result of a faulty meter which was changed in the summer. The bill she received three months later in the autumn was for £30. Maxine was pleased with British Gas when she negotiated repaying her arrears because they were very helpful and arranged a level of payment that she could afford. Her one complaint was that the people in the showroom would not let her use a telephone in there and so she was forced to use one in the street:

> *They should be able to deal with everything on their freephone in there ... specially when you've got a baby in a pushchair, you know, and you haven't got to leave them outside the callbox in the market.*

Toni was in a similar position to Maxine. She was a 28 year old lone parent with an eight month old baby. Toni received a quarterly winter bill for £70. While this may not seem particularly high, she had other commitments and so got in touch with British Gas and arranged to pay it off in weekly instalments of £9. Toni missed a couple of payments, but finally settled the account in 10 or 11 weeks. By the time her next quarterly bill arrived she was in a position to pay it all off.

Toni was aware of prepayment plans, but did not want to have to be tied down to regular payments. She liked to keep control of her money and pay her bill off as soon as possible, rather than having to find something every week for it:

> *I prefer to pay just when the bill comes, you know, straight off, sort of thing. Then I've got no debts, like, weekly.*

She did not want to have a standing order or direct debit:

> *I know there's direct debit and all that but I don't want any trouble with my bank account because I've done that with Cable and it's too much hassle to go through your bank account and that. They take out money and they send you the bill and then you don't get an estimate till later and don't know how much money's been taken out of your account. All sorts of things can go wrong.*

When she found it difficult to pay a bill, she got in touch with British Gas and negotiated a payment scheme.

Brenda, Hannah, Mavis, Maxine and Toni had all negotiated a repayment scheme with British Gas after they received a quarterly bill. In all of these cases, the bills were eventually settled and disconnection avoided, but they have all had great difficulties finding the money.

Unsuccessful payment plans

British Gas figures for the quarter ending December 1992 state that 34 per cent of all disconnection cases were the result of 'broken contact', though it would perhaps be better described as 'broken payment plans'. This highlights the fact that payment plans do not always help people avoid disconnection, but the reason for this is not necessarily because people break off contact with British Gas. One of the main reasons for the failure of payment plans to prevent disconnection is that the level of repayments is set without adequate regard to a customer's ability to pay. This is not necessarily because British Gas imposes an unrealistic level on a customer. It is more often because people are very keen to reduce their debts and so voluntarily suggest levels of repayment which are unrealistic. British Gas then accepts this figure without ascertaining the income and outgoings of the customer. Of course, some customers may find it intrusive if British Gas were to start asking questions about such financial matters, but if this information is not known, then it is virtually impossible to know whether a payment level is realistic or not. Another problem for British Gas is that what is a reasonable level may not simply be determined by income. Payments would have to exceed current consumption in order to prevent debt building up and customers may not have enough income to be able to afford to consume all that they need.

Sid went onto £23.35 a week social security hardship payments when he was made redundant in November 1991. He knew he would have difficulty with his bills, so got in touch with British Gas and asked to change from quarterly bills to a weekly payment plan:

> *But when I got the payment book, it was £8 the first time and then £9 per week; but at the time I was only getting £23 Income Support so I couldn't afford to pay that ... What they wanted off me was impossible. I could have paid them but I wouldn't have had anything to eat.*

Sid fell behind and wrote three letters to British Gas explaining his difficulties. He said that all he received from them were two letters asking for their money and enclosing new payment books, with payments revised upwards, rather than downwards.

Percy was having similar problems to Sid. He found it difficult to find instalments of £5 a week from his Invalidity Benefit:

> *I had had a chance to pay on budget. But things are hard and after I missed a couple, I went down ... they were going to cut me off for £80. They give me the letter they were going to disconnect you. And I said, 'Well, can I pay £20?' So she [member of staff at the showroom] went into the computer, this woman, and she said, 'You've had a budget account,' and she threw the money and the paper back at me, like that ... That woman did me. That was the thing that did me, when she threw*

*my money back at me and said 'You've had your chance'.
Those were her words ... and that's what upset everything.
Believe me, at the time, I would have probably tried to pay it
off, but you know how you are when you're angry ... There
were other people watching, you see. It's a bit embarrassing
– and she didn't say it quietly.*

Despite the humiliation Percy felt, he telephoned British Gas and
offered the £20 again. This offer was now accepted and he sent off the
money. He went away for two weeks and when he came back he had a bill
for the remaining £60 and a new bill for £100. He did not believe it could
be this high and, because of his recent experience in the showroom, felt he
had no option but be disconnected. Percy arranged for British Gas to come
on a particular day to disconnect him and was further enfuriated when they
arrived a day early when he was not there. Percy's whole experience has
left him bitter and determined not to pay:

I'll go to prison before I pay it.

Percy's experience demonstrates the importance of dealing sensitively
with customers when they do make contact. Percy admitted that he gets
angry easily and it may not have been easy for British Gas staff to deal with
him, but his experience in the showroom completely discouraged him from
making any further contact or payment. Percy was disconnected in June
1992 and was still disconnected four months later.

Norman had always found it difficult to manage money. After his
divorce, he lived with his mother who took care of all the household
budgeting. When she died in 1990, he knew he would have difficulties with
his bills and so went onto a prepayment plan of £15 a fortnight. He kept
up these payments until he went on short time at work in March 1992. Then
in May 1992, he became unemployed and qualified for Income Support of
£84 a fortnight:

*At the time I went out of work the car insurance, electric, gas
all came together. One daughter's 21st, the other graduated
– all just hit me in the one period of time ... That was the time
when it all came to a head.*

Norman found it difficult to cope with the situation he was in and did
not get in touch with British Gas to explain his change in circumstances and
so lower his payments. He thought he had to just keep trying to pay at the
same level. Norman was disconnected and eventually agreed to have a
token meter installed.

Trevor was vague about the details, but said that his weekly payments were 'high, given limited resources'. He claimed Income Support and, following disconnection, went on Fuel Direct.

Mike had been receiving quarterly gas bills, but found that he just could not afford them when he went onto short time and had serious difficulties with paying his mortgage. He went onto a payment plan of £55 a month, but found this very difficult to keep up. By the time he received his winter quarterly bill, he owed £170. He did nothing about this until he received a disconnection notice and then telephoned British Gas at the regional head office to say that he would now keep up his payments again. They agreed, over the telephone, not to disconnect him, but this was never put in writing and two weeks later he was disconnected by engineers from his local office:

> *I used to ring them up at Staines. That was the address and the telephone number on the letter that I used to receive ... Am I supposed to telephone that office or my local office? The letters that I received from the Gas Board, they were from the Staines office.*

High payment levels are not the only problems with payment plans. For Len, the problem with his payment plan was partly the level, but also the frequency of payment. Len received £69.40 a fortnight Income Support after deductions for water rates and poll tax. He used to receive quarterly bills:

> *I used to save it and go without and cut down [on gas] ... and other things. And then when it come I used to ... I'd probably get red, get me red reminder and I'd know I'd got to pay it up then. One year gas prices, they went up with a bump, and it were ninety odd quid to pay.*

In the past he had borrowed from friends to pay bills, but was unwilling to keep doing so. The bill for the winter quarter was £150. Len went to British Gas to ask if he could pay this bill in fortnightly instalments because this is the frequency he (along with many other people) receive their benefit cheque. The people in the showroom seemed to agree and they told him that he would have to pay an equivalent of £15 a week. This was almost half his income after deductions, but Len agreed to the level because he wanted to pay his bill.

Len paid £20 and was then sent a letter saying that he had not kept up his weekly payments. He said that it was just too difficult for him to make the weekly payments and so was disconnected. Len did not think he should have been disconnected because he had every intention of paying his bill; it was just a question of working out a suitable method:

> *Somehow, at the end of the day, whatever I owe them, they're gonna have to be repaid, aren't they? There's no getting away from that. I'm not going to get me gas for nothing.*

Len's repayments were very high given his level of income, but the frequency at which British Gas wanted him to pay his instalments also caused him difficulties. When he received the *Helpline Pack*, he sent off a card asking to pay fortnightly but heard nothing and was disconnected soon after (in July 1992). He did not remember being offered a meter, but says that he would have considered having one. Len felt that he did not make enough effort to explain his difficulties, but he did get in touch and his attempts to negotiate before disconnection failed. He saw no point in getting in touch again and was waiting to go to court as he saw this as the only way of settling the issue. He hoped that he would be reconnected for Christmas. Again this shows the importance of maintaining contact with people who do get in touch, however tentatively.

In two cases, mobility problems led to difficulties with bill paying. Audrey had to rely on friends, relatives and neighbours to pay her instalments as she was not very mobile and could not make the half hour bus journey each way to the showroom. This was not only practically difficult but also made Audrey feel very dependent on other people. Audrey disliked debt and so got anxious if the instalment was not paid, but she also did not like to worry her friends. When Audrey was in hospital for a few weeks, some of her instalments were not paid, leading her to get into debt.

Albert was 77 and also relied on neighbours to pay his bills. This caused him practical difficulties on top of the financial problem of finding the money. He was not sure how much all his bills were, but knew that he was left with £10.20 a week. When he was on a payment plan, he found it difficult to afford his gas instalments (although Albert was slightly vague and confused about this).

Audrey and Albert both got into difficulties because they paid or arranged to pay their instalments in cash at the showroom. Customers with bank accounts sometimes pay their instalments automatically by standing order or direct debit. This may seem a trouble-free method, but two families in the sample got into debt while using it. Lisa and Mark's monthly standing order to British Gas was cancelled by the bank without informing the couple. It was only after six weeks that British Gas informed the couple that two instalments had been missed and they were now coming off the payment plan. Lisa and Mark managed to avoid disconnection by setting up a new payment plan at a slightly higher rate to take the arrears into account. Lisa felt that the difficulties would not have arisen if either her bank or British Gas had informed her immediately.

Billy did get disconnected. His standing order was cancelled by the bank in November 1991 when Billy's girlfriend left. Although he eventually received reminders and letters, Billy was so immersed in his work that he took little notice of them. He actually thought they were standard statements of his account rather than notices of arrears. The first time Billy realised he was in arrears was when he received the Warrant Notice. He then got in touch with British Gas and asked for two weeks to get to the showroom and pay the £400 arrears that had accumulated. He was told to pay immediately. He was disconnected soon after.

Malcolm was adamant that he got into arrears because he was not sent a new payment book. Even so, he said he kept up his payments but that British Gas denied this as he did not have his book stamped. Malcolm got in touch a number of times requesting a new book. He maintained that his requests were ignored and he was treated in a way which soured his relationship with British Gas. He remembered one particular telephone call he had before disconnection. He said that the woman was:

> *Quite nasty, to the extent as if to say that she owned the Gas Board, 'You have to pay this bill, if you don't pay, this will happen or that will happen'. So I asked her a question. I said, 'Do you talk to your husband or your fiancé like this?' And she said, 'No'. I said, 'Well don't talk to me like that. I came on the phone for a genuine inquiry, you know, I didn't come on to be insulted' ... To be honest I was a bit short fused, lost my temper a bit, 'cos I thought I might have got a better approach of an attitude, trying to explain that I wanted a book. I wanted to pay my bill, you know. Obviously I can't obtain gas for nothing ... Her attitude wasn't very understanding, you know. It was like, 'I'm sitting on a throne' type of thing, 'looking down on you sitting on a stool', you know.*

Malcolm admitted that he did not keep his cool and he may have been a difficult customer for the member of staff to deal with, but his family were struggling to live on Income Support and he was genuinely trying to sort out his problem. He felt he was not dealt with as sensitively as the situation demanded.

Going through a major change in circumstance such as redundancy or divorce can be a traumatic experience, with emotional as well as financial consequences. Often people find it difficult to deal with the situation they are in and get in touch with their creditors. In picking up the telephone, they have to admit to themselves first of all and then to someone else, that they are having problems. This is certainly why some of those with payment plans do break off contact with British Gas.

Within a couple of months, Ray's marriage and business both fell apart. He soon found another job, but was made redundant within a year. At 36, Ray had never been unemployed and considered himself a dynamic entrepeneur. He was reluctant to claim benefits and only did so after two months, when he had absolutely nothing else to live on. Ray's wife had originally arranged for them to set up a prepayment plan in order to avoid high quarterly bills. After his redundancy, Ray got into difficulties with these payments (as well as with other bills) and could not bring himself to explain the situation to anyone:

> *I think I was bound in a world of unknown, with everything going wrong for me. You tend to shut yourself up and ... tunnel vision, into what on earth's going to happen next. Bills and things that come through the door, and threats, don't seem to have the effect that it would if you were OK.*

Ray thought it was difficult for people who are unemployed (particularly if they are unemployed for the first time), to know where to start with their financial problems. He broke contact with British Gas because he simply could not face the situation he was in.

Billy spoke of the 'emotional trauma' he went through when he split up from his girlfriend after her miscarriage. More than ever, he immersed himself in his work in order to cope with the situation. This made it difficult to deal with anything else in his life. While this was not why he got into debt, it did affect his ability to handle the situation once it arose.

Emotional upheaval not only prevents people from getting in touch at all, it also affects the way they react to contact. Percy found it extremely embarrassing and denigrating when his offer of £20 was thrown back at him in the gas showroom. This has discouraged him from future contact with British Gas and he preferred to wait for a court summons. Malcolm also admitted that he was not completely calm when he spoke to British Gas staff.

Reasons why payment plans are not set up

It is clear, then, that payment plans are not always successful in avoiding disconnection. Some people, however, are disconnected without even attempting to set up such a plan. As we shall see, the reasons for this lie to some extent in awareness of and attitudes towards payment plans. But they also lie in the characteristics of people who get into debt.

Awareness of and attitudes to payment plans

Some people did not get in touch to negotiate payment plans because they simply did not have the money to pay the bill and did not think that British Gas could, or would help. They felt that there was no point contacting British Gas unless they have some or all of the money owed. They were sometimes completely unaware, or only had some idea that payment plans were an option for them. These opinions and lack of awareness are not challenged by the first few communications sent by British Gas (original bill, red bill, warrant notice). Although these communications do mention alternative methods, customers tend to focus on the demands for payment and so their attitudes are reinforced. The *Helpline Pack* is the one communication which most obviously encourages contact, but some people were sure that they had not seen it. This may be because they never received a copy or it simply did not make any impact on them. Even when people responded to the *Helpline Pack*, for example to apply for Fuel Direct, there was not always enough time to stop disconnection.

Some people were adamant that they had not received the *Helpline Pack* (or received it only on the day of disconnection). These people were often unaware of alternatives and so believed that the only way to stop disconnection was to pay the whole bill. If they did not have the money for this, they thought that there was no point getting in touch. Not surprisingly, it was people on very low incomes who usually felt they had nothing to offer. It was often quite difficult, psychologically, for them to talk to an organisation about the problems they were having.

Susanne's financial difficulties began when she was divorced. She found it very difficult to manage and was trying to sell her house so that she could pay her mortgage arrears. She knew that her gas boiler was old and inefficient and that she would save money in the long run if she replaced it, but she could not afford to and so was left finding the money for very large bills. Susanne received a £200 bill in the winter and could not pay any of it. She then received another bill for £200 three months later. Susanne blamed herself for disconnection and felt that she should have got in touch, but at the time, she thought there was nothing she (or anyone else) could do:

> *It was my fault. I had the letters and the bills. I knew I was not paying the bill and that they would disconnect sometime, but I just couldn't face it. I couldn't pay so I didn't do anything*

... I knew what I owed, but I had no way of paying it ... I felt ashamed.

Susanne felt that if she just buried her head in the sand, all her problems would go away. She was unaware of the possibility of setting up a repayment plan to help with the arrears or a prepayment plan to prevent future arrears. She hoped that she would be able to sell her house and pay the bill in that way. But she did not sell her house and the problems did not go away – she was disconnected. Susanne cannot remember receiving a *Helpline Pack*, but felt that even if she had it would probably not have been successful in encouraging her to make contact.

Sunil did not get in touch for a similar reason:

I didn't have the money and I thought if I talked to them I would promise something. If I had promised something which I don't give them, then they will come over and say 'We will stop this [the gas supply]'.

Of course, by not getting in touch, Sunil was disconnected anyway. But he felt he may have got in touch if he had received the warrant letter or the *Helpline Pack*. He said that a letter like the warrant letter was left when the engineers disconnected him and that he never received the *Helpline Pack*. He was unaware of any alternative payment methods, but would have liked to pay his bills in advance in order to avoid the problems of finding money for a large quarterly bill.

Lack of awareness was not the only reason for people failing to set up payment plans. When Gary was having difficulties with his quarterly bill he was aware that he could set up a regular direct debit arrangement. But he disliked this method because his budget was tight and he did not want to slip into the red and incur bank charges. Gary knew that British Gas asked people to get in touch and explain if they were having problems. But he felt that the main problem he had was lack of money and British Gas could do little to resolve this:

Basically, you see, I don't think they've got much sympathy for anyone that's working – that's struggling – really. If you're struggling financially, it's, you're in an horrible situation anyway, aren't you? And, er, I don't think, whether you talk to somebody personally, or you're ticking boxes, doesn't make a hell of a difference – it's not putting money in your pocket.

When Doug had difficulties paying his gas bill in the past, he always got in touch. He had never been disconnected before. This time, however,

71

Doug knew that there was no way he could pay the bill and so felt that there was no point contacting British Gas:

> *I couldn't afford it. I couldn't afford to go down and pay the bill off. I just couldn't be bothered with them.*

Doug was on reduced Income Support after being sacked from his job for being drunk at work. He was beyond caring about what happened to him, 'You just couldn't care less in the end'. He felt that British Gas could do nothing to encourage contact:

> *They sent me letters, telling me what they were going to do – asking me to write back and get in touch ... I take no notice, 'cos whether they're harsh or sympathetic, makes no difference.*

Unable to deal with the debt situation

As we have seen, some people broke contact with British Gas because they could not cope with their financial situation. Others who used different methods of payment also found it difficult to cope and so did not get in touch at all.

Gary expressed a similar view to Ray when he explained why he was reluctant to get in touch with British Gas:

> *It's not very nice telling somebody that – a total stranger you don't know – that, like, I'm having financial difficulties ... I just don't want to discuss my financial – I mean you always think to yourself, I mean I always think to myself, well maybe next week I'll get some money and pay it off ... It's not very nice to say, 'Yeah, OK, I'm broke'. You're kind of having to admit you're a failure ... There's nothing I can say to them. What can I say? I can't offer them anything yet, so I just thought, 'Well, OK, let them get on with it', you know?*

John suffered stress due to the demands of his job, but when he left his job, he found himself under more financial pressures. He said he found it difficult to see things clearly at this time.

By avoiding contact with British Gas, these people may appear to staff to be deliberately avoiding payment. This is a false assumption and one which can cause people even greater distress than they are already suffering.

In a slightly different way Isobel and her co-tenants were not able to deal with their situation. They did not get in touch with British Gas because it was the responsibility of their landlord to pay their bills and he had always done so in the past. They felt that it was nothing to do with them, even though they were the ones who eventually suffered disconnection. After disconnection, they felt that they should have made more of an effort to get in touch with their landlord, but they knew that he was a busy man and did not like to worry him. When British Gas arrived to disconnect them, they explained that it was the landlord's duty to pay, but were told they would be disconnected anyway.

Absence from home

Temporary absence from home has already been identified as one of the main reasons why five people got into debt. We know that another three people who were disconnected without a payment plan were away from home for an extended period and were not available to be interviewed. It may seem that there is little that can be done to prevent debts arising in these situations but if people are aware of prepayment plans and have enough foresight, setting up such a plan by standing order or direct debit would help. Unfortunately, some people are not aware of such plans, or do not think to go on one. When they return home, some of them have enough money to pay the whole bill. If they return home before the debt recovery cycle has reached disconnection, they will still be able to avoid it. Others who return home before disconnection may not have enough money to pay it in time and so will need help. For these people, a repayment plan would be useful.

Margaret was disconnected when she was in Scotland for seven months, visiting sick relatives. She had a lot of personal worries on her mind and found it difficult to think about gas bills and other such matters. She said that she asked a friend to pay her monthly repayments when she was in Scotland, but she was not clear about the amount she left. She found herself disconnected when she returned.

Rosa was away in South America every summer and it seems that her sister lived in her flat for that time. Rosa did not speak English very well and found it difficult to communicate on the telephone. She did not find it easy to read letters. It seems that Rosa was disconnected when she was abroad and her sister managed to get her reconnected before she returned.

Eddy was disconnected because he was working away from home and did not have his post attended to. He came home after disconnection and took full responsibility for being cut off. He was aware of prepayment plans and felt that he should get organised to go on a direct debit scheme.

Frank was away from home every week. He remembered receiving bills and letters, but paid little attention to these, as he had 'other things' on his mind. His absence from home made it more difficult to get in touch with British Gas, but he accepted that he should have avoided disconnection by sorting out his affairs more successfully.

Disorganised bill-paying

Some people, like Frank perhaps, were very disorganised about bill paying. They did not negotiate a payment plan because they believed the bill had been paid. Andy was one such case. He thought he had paid his gas bill. After disconnection, he thought that he must have confused his domestic gas bill with the one he had for his pub. He disliked dealing with paperwork and so threw away many pieces of mail without reading them carefully. He did not realise he had not paid his bill until he was disconnected.

Dan and Jeff both thought they had paid their bill, and that possibly the cheque they sent must have bounced or got lost in the post. But they did remember receiving reminders or any other communication. They just did not really think they would be disconnected, or at least, not as soon as they were. They were now very careful to avoid disconnection.

Gopal received quarterly bills and said that he always paid them when he received the red reminder. In the winter of 1992, he received a bill for £190. This was slightly higher than expected, but Gopal and his wife put this down to increases in gas prices. They put the bill away and waited for the red bill to arrive. No red bill arrived and they forgot about their bill. The next communication they received was the summer bill for £70 plus the £190 owed. Again they waited for the red bill. At this time, Gopal had other things on his mind particularly his mortgage which was not much less than his salary. He said that the next communication from British Gas was disconnection itself. However, British Gas procedures for sending out original bills and subsequent reminders are automated and so it seems very strange that Gopal received two original bills and no follow-up communications. But Gopal is adamant that he received no red letters, no warrant notices, no disconnection letters and no *Helpline Packs*. As he argued:

> *The problem comes when the customer says, 'I have received no communications' and the supplier says he has sent all the communications he is supposed to send to arrive at this stage.*

Gopal still felt that disconnection could have been avoided if the people who came to disconnect him had accepted a cheque for the amount. He did not have enough cash on him to pay the whole bill and the engineers would not wait for his wife to go to the bank and withdraw the money.

15   Token meters and Fuel Direct

When payment plans are unsuccessful or customers do not get in touch with British Gas, there is a final safety net which should prevent people from being disconnected. This is the offer of a token meter and in some cases, Fuel Direct, where arrears for fuel bills are deducted at source from social security payments.

Fuel Direct is available only to some people who receive benefits. Eligibility is therefore restricted and, among those eligible, awareness is limited. Those who are eligible and aware of Fuel Direct are not always keen to use the scheme.

Everyone is eligible for a prepayment meter, regardless of income. Prepayment token meters are offered to all customers through the *Helpline Pack* as well as towards the end of the pre-disconnection debt recovery process – in the letter which notifies people of British Gas's application for a warrant of entry. Prepayment meters will be refused only if it is unsafe or impracticable to install them. Otherwise, all who request one will be given one, even if they have paid no money towards their current bill. The problems, according to British Gas, is, again, that people do not contact them and request a meter even though they are offered one. There were various reasons why some people did not request a prepayment meter. Some were unaware of the possibility of having a token meter and some were aware, but disliked the idea of having one. There is some evidence that people did request meters before disconnection, but were still disconnected.

There are three hurdles to jump to go onto Fuel Direct or to getting a meter. First of all people have to be aware of the possibility, then they have to want to take advantage of the option, then they have to be eligible. People do not always fit these criteria and are subsequently disconnected.

Awareness of token meters and Fuel Direct
In theory, everyone is offered a token meter and informed about Fuel Direct. In practice, people were not always aware of these possibilities and those who were aware did not always remember being offered them. Even when

people were aware of prepayment meters and Fuel Direct, various attitudes prevent them from requesting or applying for them.

Lack of awareness of different methods of payment was common among those disconnected. The main way in which British Gas seeks to inform people in debt about their options is through the *Helpline Pack*. But the *Helpline Pack* arrives at a fairly late stage in the debt recovery process and its message is obscured by previous communications which all emphasise payment of money. Although the timing of the *Helpline Pack* could be a problem, a more serious issue is whether people receive a pack at all. Of the 33 households in the sample who were disconnected, 10 were adamant that they did not receive the *Helpline Pack*. All three of the Asian families in the sample who had been disconnected were convinced that they had not received the *Helpline Pack* and were unaware of the existence of token meters and Fuel Direct. A further 11 of those disconnected did not remember receiving the *Helpline Pack*, but could not say for sure that they had not received it. A further three thought they had received it but were not sure. Only nine people were sure they received it. Even if these findings merely reflect a failure of memory rather than a failure by British Gas to send a *Helpline Pack*, they illustrate that the *Helpline Pack* is not making the impact British Gas would hope.

All those who did not remember seeing a *Helpline Pack* or other communications were shown copies and asked for comments. Sid did not receive a *Helpline Pack*, but after being shown one by the interviewer, he thought it might have made a difference. Wendy was sure she did not receive a *Helpline Pack*. She took the advice of her probation officer to wait for a meter, but said that if she had received the *Helpline Pack* she would have got in touch and asked to go onto Fuel Direct. Sunil also did not get a *Helpline Pack* and said that, if he had received it, he would certainly have found out more about Fuel Direct:

> *That way you are paying in advance. They are getting their money in advance and there is no chance of cutting me off ... The other way, after three months you get a bill. It can be £180. My God, how am I going to pay it?*

Sunil was also unaware of gas token meters. He felt that this would also be a good way of paying for his gas as he would be able to buy token keys when he had the money and so would not worry about finding the money for his quarterly bill. When he was reconnected, Sunil was still on Income Support and still receiving quarterly bills.

Andy disliked dealing with mail and threw out anything which looked like direct marketing. He thought that he might have thrown the *Helpline*

Pack out because at first glance he would have assumed it was promotional literature for something like a power shower. Margaret shared a letter box with a neighbour and thought that, in her case, the neighbour might have thrown the pack out because it looked a bit like a circular. This may seem difficult to believe when the message on the envelope reads:

> *The occupier of this property must act on the contents of this envelope,*

but various companies use equally strong language to entice people to open their direct mail. Some companies stamp URGENT on their envelopes to encourage people to deal with the contents as soon as possible. They may even disguise their envelopes so that they look official in order to encourage people to open and read them.

Attitudes to token meters and Fuel Direct

Lack of awareness is not the only reason why some people do not go onto Fuel Direct or get a meter. Some were aware of these options, but did not wish to take advantage of them.

Maxine disliked the idea of going onto Fuel Direct:

> *I like to handle my own money. I don't want them handling my money for me. I like to be in control.*

Margaret had money deducted from her benefit to pay for electricity. She did not want to go on the scheme for her gas bill because in the past she had found herself paying a large proportion of her benefit after using a lot of electricity. She preferred the idea of a meter to Fuel Direct because she knew exactly how much she was using and how much she was paying. But Margaret did not want a meter because she knew it would mean taking her three children out with her every time to buy tokens.

Len was already having money deducted from his benefit for water rates and poll tax. He did not want any more money deducted in this way as it meant he lost control of his spending. A meter would have allowed Len to retain control and although he was keen on the idea now he was not aware of meters before disconnection.

Gary was aware that he could have a gas prepayment meter, but did not like the idea as he was not very happy with using a prepayment meter for his electricity supply. The main problem was travelling to buy tokens. Each time he had some money for tokens he had to make another trip to buy them. Running out of tokens was a constant worry. He felt that since it is easier to cope without gas for a while than without electricity, he might not worry about buying tokens for his gas meter and so he would deprive himself of gas to avoid travelling for tokens.

Terry disliked meters for a similar reason. He knew that he spent any money he had very quickly and that if he had a meter he would never have enough money left over for tokens. He much preferred paying for his gas with Fuel Direct because then he knew that whatever money he had in his hands could be spent how he liked.

Malcolm did not want a meter because he was worried about being tempted to use the informal economy, where tokens were cheaper:

> *You can obtain the plastic tokens from people round the doors, 'off the back of a lorry', if you like, and it means that if you use them tokens and you got found out, that's it, you're prosecuted, you know. So I thought that wasn't a good idea, I'd rather do it legitimately.*

Malcolm remembered receiving a letter about a meter. He thought that the letter was not asking him if he wanted a meter, but telling him he had no choice but to have one. He therefore avoided replying to this.

Arranging installation of a token meter

After falling behind with his payments, Sid asked to have a meter installed. In theory, almost everyone is eligible for a prepayment meter. If requested, it is only refused where it would be unsafe or impracticable to install one. In practice, this does not always seem to be the case. Sid was told that he could only have a prepayment meter once he had paid off his arrears:

> *The only time they mentioned it [a meter], was when I got in touch with them the last time. They put me down for it, but they said I could only have it if the bill has been paid in full.*

Sid could not afford to pay his arrears and so was disconnected. After about a week, Sid received a letter from PSI about the research and he got in touch with British Gas to say that he would be giving an interview. He had a token meter installed soon after without paying the whole bill. Sid felt that disconnection could have been avoided if British Gas had given him a token meter sooner:

> *Why couldn't they have just done that to start with?*

According to British Gas's policy, inability to repay arrears is not a reason to make a customer ineligible for a meter. It seems, therefore, that Sid was not ineligible for a meter, but was unsuccessful in getting one because practice at the local level was at variance with national policy.

While supply of token meters is no longer the problem it once was, British Gas do not have an unlimited quantity of token meters and there may have been some problem in finding one for Sid. If this was the case, then disconnection could have been postponed while a meter was found.

John was on reduced Income Support after being advised to give up his job due to ill health. He found it difficult to cope with things in his life and when he got behind with his gas bill, he did not know what to do. Although he liked the idea of having a token meter, he was under the impression that he would have to pay all his arrears off first before one was installed. He could not afford to do this. John had not got in touch with British Gas to confirm this because he found it very difficult to deal with these situations. He was a nervous, anxious man and was waiting for a community worker to come back from holiday to help him sort things out:

> *If they are prepared to say, 'Well, look, we shall put in this here, install this meter ... we will include the present arrears as well as the meter and the meter will pay this off on the token meter', I am prepared to do this, but unfortunately I haven't asked them if they're going to agree to it or not ... I'm most confused about how they deal with these things. I do not know.*

Albert had practical and financial difficulties with his payment plan and was advised by some ex-colleagues (he used to work as a messenger for British Gas), that it was best for him to to have a prepayment meter. He said that British Gas were 'pleased to see' him when he went to ask for a token meter and he was present when it was installed. He picked up £5 worth of tokens when he collected his pension every week and found this much more convenient than having to rely on neighbours. Albert did not consider himself a disconnection case, but he was recorded in British Gas figures as such.

Arranging Fuel Direct

Eligibility for Fuel Direct is more restricted and less clear than eligibility for token meters. The decision to include someone in the scheme is made by a member of the Department of Social Security staff, not British Gas. People are included if it is deemed to be in their best interests. In order to get on the scheme, a customer has to have built up arrears of at least £42.45, and be receiving Income Support from which a weekly sum can be deducted. Some other benefits, such as Unemployment Benefit and Invalidity Benefit are included in the scheme, but only when claimants receive them in combination with Income Support.

Audrey claimed Invalidity Benefit and her daughter made enquiries about Fuel Direct with the Department of Social Security and British Gas and was told that Audrey was ineligible for the scheme because she was not in arrears. Although Audrey said that she did not deliberately get into debt to go on Fuel Direct, she was reliant on her daughter to organise her bill-paying while in hospital and her daughter may have engineered this.

From the moment he had difficulties, Terry wanted to go on Fuel Direct. He was already having money deducted from his benefit for rent, water rates, poll tax and electricity. He knew how the system worked and was fairly happy with it. He spoke and wrote to British Gas who advised him to contact the Department of Social Security. Terry contacted the Department of Social Security and they told him he would have to get disconnected before he would be able to go on Fuel Direct. He asked British Gas for a letter to say that he would be disconnected and they said he would receive one in due course. When he received the letter he took it to the DSS who then processed his application, but it was not accepted until after he was disconnected. Loss of his gas supply did not worry Terry too much, but he was annoyed that he had to pay the £34 reconnection charge:

> *I got all the proper notices and I was going down at the same time to the gas place and saying, 'take it out of my dole', and then going to the DSS who said, 'we can't, you have to get chopped off' ... In their eyes they can't take it out of your benefit until something urgent comes up like you get chopped off.*

So some people want to go on Fuel Direct or get a meter and believe that the best (or only way) to achieve this is to accumulate debt and get disconnected.

Sid got into difficulties with his payment plan when he was asked to pay £8 a week from his £23.35 reduced Income Support. He then applied to the Department of Social Security for Fuel Direct and was bemused when he was told he would only have to pay £5.25 from his benefit. He felt that this was more reasonable than the figure British Gas was quoting. Although Sid was happy to move onto Unemployment Benefit (of £46.10 a week), this meant that he was no longer eligible for Fuel Direct:

> *They said it was Unemployment Benefit – they couldn't deduct. It had nothing to do with them, it was private. They couldn't deduct the money ... I felt a bit sick.*

So Sid had to pay the amount specified by British Gas. This amount was then increased by British Gas to £9 a week and then £12 a week and caused great difficulties for Sid.

Others tried to arrange Fuel Direct before disconnection, but only succeeded in getting onto the scheme afterwards. Trevor, John and Ben used a form they received with the *Helpline Pack* to ask for Fuel Direct. All three were nevertheless disconnected although they were put on the scheme after disconnection. Those who do apply to the Department of Social Security to go on the scheme before disconnection often wait some time before their forms are processed and they are accepted. Although British Gas should allow extra time (up to three weeks) before disconnecting these people, they know if someone has applied for Fuel Direct only if the customer tells British Gas. In practice, people who applied for Fuel Direct were sometimes disconnected before they heard whether they had been accepted onto the scheme.

Using disconnection to get preferred payment method

Wendy did not get in touch with British Gas because she was advised by her probation officer that she would be better off paying for her gas by prepayment meter and that the only way to get a token meter was by first being disconnected. It is not clear how the probation officer formed this opinion, but it is one that needs challenging.

Audrey said that she did not deliberately get herself disconnected in order to go onto Fuel Direct, but her daughter may have deliberately engineered Audrey's disconnection in order to get her onto the scheme which suited her so well.

16   The experience of disconnection

Thirty-three of the forty-five households in the study had been disconnected. In order to understand the reasons for contact and non-contact after disconnection, it is important to look at the experience these people went through. In fact many people felt that, at least in principle, British Gas was justified in disconnecting them because they had not paid their gas bills. Eddy said:

> *It was my fault for not paying the bill, so you can't blame anyone except myself.*

Sunil agreed:

> *You are using someone else's stuff and they cut you off - that is fair. They have the right to do that ... It's their money and I have to pay them. Simple ... It's my fault. I didn't pay and I could have asked for help.*

Jeff expressed a similar view:

> *I had a bill to pay and I didn't pay it, so it is fair enough that they should try and get me to pay it. In that case I admit that I was wrong.*

Although people felt that British Gas was right, in theory, to disconnect them, the way that disconnection took place in practice was often criticised. Dave, who claimed he was disconnected by mistake, was very disturbed by the experience of disconnection. In common with many men in the sample, he was particularly upset about the fact that his property was entered without his permission:

> *I'm not so much bothered about the disconnection and all that – it's an inconvenience and I can manage all that. It's the thought that a private company can just walk into your house while you're out and pick your lock, which is virtually breaking and entering ... Even the police if they come have to knock on the door.*

Dave was also angry that no card was left to explain that he had been disconnected. He also suspected that British Gas engineers deliberately waited until his family had left the premises, as the family had only been out for one hour the whole day and it was during that period that they were disconnected. He felt that the whole experience was similar to being burgled – entry without permission:

It's just the thought that that these people from the Gas Board ... they could just lurk about until you went out, and then break into your house, and pick the lock on the house, and walk into your house, and spend an hour in here – yeah? – while you're out and then just waltz off without leaving a letter, a note or a card or anything. Nothing ... It's horrible.

Susanne's partner, Tom, was also surprised that British Gas could enter the premises without permission. The act of disconnection was again seen as similar to burglary:

They broke in, took the meter. If I broke into somebody's house, I'd be locked up!

Ray felt very strongly about this issue:

The only thing that I've got to say that I did not agree with – I was out of the house when they came in to disconnect the gas. So somebody's actually come into my home, without my permission and disconnected the gas – that, I got very, very, very upset about that.

With 14 years of unemployment behind him, Len felt disregarded by society. His experience of gas disconnection contributed to the alienation he felt:

Well, I just thought, 'What am I then? Am I a third class citizen?' I think they've just got contempt because I'm on the bottom – but where do I go from here? ... I don't think they should have that power [to enter without permission]. It's like everything else, it puts them above the law – because they've got the money, and the money says, 'I can do this'. And money shouldn't have that sway.

Billy was concerned by the fact that his daughter might have been at home on her own when British Gas arrived to disconnect him:

I was pissed off about that, I really was. Very cheesed that somebody had come in. If you had a 12 year old daughter –

> *what happens if she had gotten back from school and she was*
> *upstairs. Her instruction from me is not to answer the door.*
> *So she doesn't answer the door and the guy comes through the*
> *door and cuts the gas off. Is this a good idea? No, it is not a*
> *good idea and I would personally have clubbed the man. This*
> *is not on. There should be a different type of thing ... It makes*
> *me very angry that my daughter could have been frightened.*

Percy saw the letter which gave him the date for disconnection and he made sure that he could be present. However, British Gas arrived the day before they said they would and Percy was not there. Percy's neighbours saw what was happening and knew where Percy was, so got in touch immediately and Percy came 'flying down' to see what was happening:

> *'What you doing here? You're not supposed to come until*
> *tomorrow'. He said, 'I don't know about it'. He were nice,*
> *the bloke, don't get me wrong. He had a locksmith with him.*

Percy received a locksmith's bill which he felt he should not have to pay. The whole experience left him angry and did nothing to encourage him to pay his bill, quite the reverse:

> *I'll go to prison before I pay it.*

Gopal was actually present when British Gas came to disconnect him. He was willing to give a cheque to the engineers in order to avoid disconnection. According to British Gas, when their engineers are offered a cheque in such circumstances, they check the records they have with them and only refuse a cheque if previous cheques have bounced. In Gopal's case, the engineers told him that they would only accept cash and could not wait for Gopal's wife to go and draw some out from their bank account:

> *I feel very upset about it because my wife told him, 'If you can,*
> *give me some time, I can get the money and I will pay you' ...*
> *He said, 'If you have the cash, produce it or I disconnect' ...*
> *Normally in this country you do not keep cash at home.*

Attitude of British Gas staff following disconnection
There was a feeling among some people that the reaction of British Gas staff changed once they had been disconnected. Tariq says that he felt 'bitter' about disconnection:

> *The Gas Board ... they're not much helpful when you're*
> *disconnected. They treat you like criminals.*

After Malcolm was disconnected he telephoned British Gas immediately to try and get reconnected. He said he:

> *... felt stupid, felt though I was begging. Felt I'd failed.*

Dan said:

> *They were condescending, like, because I had been cut off.*

But he felt that there may be an explanation for this:

> *At first she was kind of, like, rude. But I think this was because she was expecting me to be rude. In the end she was OK.*

Even so, 19 people did manage to get their gas supply reconnected soon after disconnection.

17 Reconnection

Acording to British Gas figures, during the quarter ending December 1992 20 per cent of people who had had their gas supply disconnected were reconnected within a month. Of the 33 households that had been disconnected in our study, 25 had been in touch with British Gas within two weeks and 19 had their supply reconnected soon afterwards. A further eight households had been reconnected after periods of up to five months without their gas.

In some instances they had the money to pay but did not pay, although seldom was it a case of wilful non-payment. Most, however, did not have the money to pay but were forced to find it from somewhere because it was so difficult to live without gas. This money was acquired from a variety of sources such as borrowing, opting for voluntary redundancy, and by getting into debt with other commitments such as rent. But for the great majority it was a question of opting for Fuel Direct or a token meter.

Finding the money

Four people had got in touch soon after disconnection because they had the money to pay their arrears. It seems unlikely that these people were deliberate non-payers. Absence from home and disorganised bill-paying seem more plausible explanations.

Eddy had been working away from home and had been unaware that he owed any money. When he returned to find himself disconnected he went to the showroom and paid his bill. It is likely that this study underestimates the number of people in Eddy's position as these highly mobile people are the most difficult for interviewers to contact.

Gopal had enough money to pay his bills but said he had not received any reminders or disconnection letters and so forgot to pay. He realised he was in debt only when he was disconnected and so paid his bill immediately.

In Amit's case, he did not pay his bill because he had been too busy to pick it up from his tenants' house. Disconnection spurred his tenants to get in touch with him and he paid the bill immediately.

Andy thought he had paid his bill and took little notice of any British Gas letters. It was only when he was disconnected that he realised he had not paid, so he went to the showroom immediately and paid all the money owed. Although Andy said that his disconnection was solely due to disorganisation, he may have been delaying payment and misjudged the day on which he would be disconnected.

A number of others were prompted by the difficulties of living without gas to find the money to repay the arrears in full. Following disconnection they could no longer bury their heads in the sand and they could no longer ignore the situation they were in. Having children often made people place a high level of importance on restoring the gas supply and they raised the money to repay the arrears in any way they could.

These households had found the money by borrowing, by spending their redundancy money or by going without or getting into debt with other bills. They were not deliberate non-payers. Nor were their financial problems solved by payment of their gas bill arrears. They might have paid off those arrears, but only at the cost of owing someone else. Sometimes people raised the money in these ways because they were unaware of the alternative methods of payment. Sometimes it was because they did not want to pay by other methods.

Sunil thought that he should have got in touch with British Gas before disconnection to explain his situation, but he felt he had nothing to offer. Once he was disconnected, he realised that he had to do something because his family (including his two year old son) were heavily dependent on gas for cooking, heating and hot water. Sunil did not know about alternative methods of payment such as a prepayment meter or Fuel Direct. He was only aware of weekly or monthly payment plans and stamps. While Sunil remembered receiving the original bill, red bill and disconnection letter, he did not remember seeing a *Helpline Pack* and said that the warrant letter was left when he was disconnected. It is not surprising, then, that he thought that the only way he could get his gas supply back was to pay his bill. Since he did not have the money himself, he borrowed money from friends and was subsequently reconnected.

Salim's experience was very similar. His son, Tariq, got in touch before disconnection to ask for more time to pay, but soon after, they were disconnected. They received a reminder and disconnection letter, but no *Helpline Pack*. They were unaware of any alternative methods of payment except direct debit. When they were disconnected, Tariq went to the showroom to offer £400 (of the £700-£800 bill) and explained that there were seven children in the household, one of whom was blind. He was told that he would still have to pay the whole bill before reconnection and so was forced to borrow the extra money to get reconnected.

Billy usually had enough money to pay his monthly gas instalments, but got into difficulties when his standing order was cancelled by the bank. He did not realise for some months, by which time his bill amounted to £400. This was still not an enormous amount for Billy and he had every intention of paying, but needed a few weeks to get his salary and get to a showroom. He did not get this time and was disconnected. After disconnection, Billy borrowed money from a friend, knowing that within a couple of weeks he would be able to repay his friend in full. Billy was aware of alternative methods of paying for his gas, but knew that he usually had enough money to pay his bill.

Mohammed got in touch soon after disconnection to pay his bill. In order to find the money, he borrowed some and got behind with his rent and electricity payments. Mohammed went to the showroom with £200 to repay his arrears. He was told that this was not enough because he would have to pay for all gas consumed to date, another £100, before he could be reconnected. Mohammed protested that he had not received the first bill for this, let alone any reminder. He was told that the bill would be posted to him that day and it would have to be paid. Mohammed was angry because it had been difficult enough to find £200. He knew he would not be able to raise another £100 and, in any case, he felt that it was unfair that, as he saw it, he had to pay a bill he had not even seen. Mohammed and his family tried to live without gas for a while. It was summer, so heating was not essential and they bought a cheap second-hand electric cooker to keep them going. They used a kettle to boil water. Eventually, they managed to save up enough to pay the new bill too, but the experience has left them bitter:

> *They didn't want to know. They wanted us to pay the new bill. We said, 'We haven't even got it in the post yet!' They said it was ready to be sent out. I said, 'Fine. Let's get us back on first'. They said, 'No. You've got to pay the new bill.' ... We thought the gas people treated us very bad in the way of the last repayment of the bill – that was terrible. I couldn't believe it. I couldn't believe it.*

They were given no alternative but to pay the arrears and the new bill in cash. Partly because of this, Mohammed's wife, Jenny, was also quite scathing about the *Helpline Pack*:

> *It clearly says on the paper, 'If you're having any difficulty, please let us know, blah, blah, blah', and when you do that*

they actually refuse, 'You can't pay like that or like that. You pay cash or nothing at all'. ... When you get in touch, no-one wants to listen. This is the problem. They only want to know – 'have you paid all the amount, or no?' They don't want to listen to your problem, and it is bad. They should listen to my problem.

They felt that the *Helpline Pack* gave a false impression:

It's a lie. It's an illusion. I mean, a customer looks at that, yeah? And it sounds good. It sounds brilliant. But when you ring up, they say, 'No you can't. You can't have that scheme'. So, in the end, how are they helping you in paying the bill?

In a sense, Mohammed and Jenny were not being asked to pay 'a new bill', but to pay all their arrears. They had already consumed the gas and so had to pay for it before they could be reconnected. While this is standard practice for British Gas, it was seen quite differently by Mohammed and Jenny.

Susanne had avoided contact before disconnection because she just could not face up to the difficulty she was in. She thought that British Gas could do nothing to help her and so just tried to forget about her problems, hoping that they would go away. She did not remember receiving the *Helpline Pack*, but felt that, even if she had received it, it probably would have made no difference. Once she was disconnected, Susanne could no longer pretend to herself that everything was fine. Even so, she still found it difficult to cope with the situation and relied on her new partner to help. He went to the showroom on her behalf and paid her £35 reconnection charge. He also found out that Susanne could have a meter and since she could not find the money to pay all her arrears, he arranged for one to be installed.

Fuel Direct and token meters

The largest group, 13 households in all, negotiated reconnection by agreeing to repay their arrears through either Fuel Direct or a token meter calibrated to collect arrears as future gas is consumed. Some of these had asked to change before they were disconnected.

Terry had informed both the Department of Social Security and British Gas of his wish to go onto Fuel Direct as soon as he got into difficulties. He had been in touch four times with British Gas asking to go onto Fuel Direct. He was referred to the DSS who told him he would have to be disconnected first. He was disconnected and then went onto Fuel Direct.

Soon after receiving the *Helpline Pack*, Ben telephoned British Gas to ask for more time to pay his bill as he was having difficulties. At the same time he sent off a form saying that he was on Income Support and would like to go onto Fuel Direct. Six days later, Ben was disconnected and only subsequently succeeded in arranging Fuel Direct.

Audrey's daughter had asked British Gas and the Department of Social Security if she could go onto Fuel Direct before disconnection, but they told her that she must have arrears. After disconnection, Audrey's daughter went back to the DSS and British Gas and arranged for her to go on Fuel Direct. She was reconnected within a couple of days.

Albert asked for a prepayment meter before disconnection, but apparently only received one afterwards. Wendy did not get in touch with British Gas because her probation officer advised her to get disconnected so that she could get a token meter. This is what she did and she now had a meter.

For others, the need to reconnect their gas supply made them realise that they should change their payment method, even if they did not really want to. Typically, these people were elderly, disabled or had children and so felt it is very important to keep their gas supply.

Nick did not want a token meter, but after running up arrears on his payment plan, he was given no alternative. Nick needed the gas supply reconnected for the sake of his two children and so accepted the token meter. He still felt that if he left his house he might be able to get away without repaying all his arrears.

Mike and his wife did not want a token meter and so tried to borrow money from friends when they were disconnected. But when they got in touch with British Gas, they were asked to pay a £350 deposit on top of their £700 bill. They knew that they would not be able to borrow this much money from friends and so reluctantly accepted a token meter.

Norman did not want a token meter at first:

I didn't fancy putting myself out to get the tokens.

But when he was disconnected he realised he had no choice but to get one. He now had a half hour bus journey each way (which cost him a total of £1.40) to buy tokens. British Gas was about to send him a book so that he could buy them from his local post office.

It may seem that token meters solve debt problems as it is impossible for people to use gas that they cannot afford. While it is true that prepayment meters prevent people from getting into arrears, they certainly do not solve the more fundamental fuel debt problem of guaranteeing that people can afford adequate warmth.

Wendy managed to get her token meter after disconnection, but she was unable to afford all the gas she needed for herself and her baby. She heated up water for her baby's bath in a twin tub and visited friends to share the warmth of their homes. When she was disconnected, she went to stay with some friends 15 miles from her home. When Wendy has paid off her arrears through the token meter, she will no longer appear as a statistic on fuel debt. It is also virtually impossible for her ever to be disconnected again. Officially, she will disappear as a cause for concern. Unofficially, Wendy's fuel poverty will probably persist. Problems like Wendy's are highlighted in the recent study of *Hidden disconnections* (Community Energy Research and Birmingham Settlement, 1993).

Due to technical difficulties, British Gas has lagged behind the electricity companies in developing prepayment meters. Recently, however, British Gas has developed the Quantum prepayment meter which uses a secure smart card (the GASCARD) instead of coins or tokens. British Gas may be able to reduce the number of disconnections by offering these meters more readily, but it should be remembered that disconnection statistics are only one indicator of fuel poverty. And increasing the supply of meters will not tackle the demand side issue that some people do not want a prepayment meter.

Likewise, there can be problems for people on Fuel Direct. While there is an official limit to how much money can be deducted from benefit, more can be deducted if people are willing. Terry was *not* on reduced Income Support, but received only about £20 a fortnight in benefit. This was because he had accumulated rent, electricity, gas and poll tax arrears in the past and was paying them off through direct deductions from his benefit. A single person of Terry's age (20) is entitled to Income Support of £33.60 a week. From this, Terry had the following deducted each week;

Rent and water rates	£3.31
Electricity	£6.50
Gas	£9.50
Poll tax	£4.50

This comes to a total of £23.81 a week, leaving him with £9.79 a week to buy food, clothes and other household items as well as paying travelling costs (for example to Jobcentres and job interviews). Deductions can range up to 25 per cent of weekly benefit, or more where the claimant agrees to lose more to escape debt. In Terry's case, it seems he must have (perhaps unwillingly or unwittingly) volunteered to have this large amount deducted from his benefit. If he complained about it, the amount would probably have to be reduced. But Terry had mixed feelings about it. On one level he knew that he was not good at budgeting and managing his money. Direct deductions therefore provided a service to him. As he said, he was:

> *... lazy with payments ... and not very capable of keeping my money and that, you know, paying gas bills and all that.*

Direct deductions therefore 'save hassle'. But he also laughed at the way he had to live on less than two pounds a day and said it was 'hideous'. Of course, it would be virtually impossible for Terry to survive on this alone and so he resorted to doing a few 'fiddle jobs' to supplement his income.

> *You turn to crime, that's what happens, you turn to crime.*

Terry also relied on his girlfriend, Claire, who received Income Support payments of £67 a week as a lone parent with a six month old baby. Whereas the income from his 'fiddle jobs' was variable, Claire's income was regular. Their entitlement to benefit was assessed separately as Claire was officially living on her own while on the council's waiting list and so qualified as a lone parent. In practice, she spent most of the time at Terry's flat and shared her income with him.

Although Terry was surviving (albeit through crime and 'defrauding' the Department of Social Security through his undeclared living arrangements), he was worried that the DSS would think that he was managing on £19 a fortnight and felt that this was an adequate amount of money to pay people to live. This seems to imply that he was unaware that the DSS had no right to expect him to live on this and could only deduct such a high proportion of his benefit if they had his *consent* to it.

Malcolm was generally happy with Fuel Direct as he wanted to clear his arrears and felt relieved that British Gas were guaranteed to receive their money. But he also found it difficult to afford the money deducted from his benefit. He used to pay £6 or £7 a week when he was on a payment plan, but now the Department of Social Security were deducting £14 a week from his benefit:

> *By all means take money off you, but leave you with something. You have to eat, you have to wear clothes ... It wasn't myself I was thinking of, it was basically the kids.*

Government figures show that in August 1992, between one in eight and one in four of Income Support claimants were receiving less to live on each week than the basic benefit rate as a result of direct deductions. More than 300,000 claimants were having deductions specifically for fuel arrears.

Living without a gas supply was not easy and yet some British Gas procedures tended to prolong the experience. Jeff criticised British Gas for asking him to pay a £250 deposit before reconnecting him. He was left without any hot water, heating or cooking facilities:

> *I was disgusted and I thought, 'Well I don't really want to continue my sort of account with British Gas'. I was ill, actually ill, that weekend because I couldn't raise the money. Like ill, on my own here without any gas – you know what I mean? And I was really disgusted, you know. They really came down on me ... It was immobilising really. I was left with nothing to cook with or wash with ... It was terrible, absolutely terrible. I was ill and I was dirty and starving as well, because then I didn't even have a kettle ... I was disgusted really. It was a lot of money that they were asking me to pay. They broke into my house.*

A general complaint was that British Gas would not reconnect supplies at the weekend. For those who were disconnected on a Thursday or Friday and paid up immediately, it was annoying that they had to last a weekend without a supply.

18   Long-term disconnection

As we have seen, British Gas statistics show that the majority of people who are disconnected have not been reconnected within a month. Some of these will have moved permanently or may be living away from home for an extended period. Indeed there were at least 13 households who had been disconnected and whom we failed to interview for these reasons.

Altogether, seven of the households where interviews did take place were without gas for more than a month. In some cases they had felt there was little point in contacting British Gas, because they still had no money to pay the arrears. In other instances they *had* been in touch, but were unsuccessful in arranging reconnection.

Nothing to offer
Just as people had not made contact *before* disconnection because they felt they had to pay in full but could not raise the money, there were those who felt the same way even after disconnection. Usually they were either unaware of the possibility of paying by Fuel Direct or prepayment meter or they did not want to use them. They were often people without children and they felt they could manage without gas, especially during the summer months when they were interviewed.

Gary did not get in touch with British Gas either before or soon after disconnection because he did not have enough money to pay the arrears. He and his partner had an electric cooker and immersion heater and so it was not a great hardship to go without gas during the summer. Five months after disconnection, Gary used his redundancy money and borrowed from friends to get reconnected.

Doug was in a similar position. He had no money to pay his bill and was only vaguely aware of token meters. He lived on his own and had an electric cooker and water heating, but no other electric heating. He felt that there was no point getting in touch with British Gas.

Unsuccessful attempts to negotiate with British Gas
Ibrahim was in touch with British Gas before disconnection, but had not been since. His earlier attempts to solve his problems were unsuccessful

and he saw no reason why he should have more success now. Ibrahim knew about token meters but did not want one. His health was not very good and he would find it difficult to get out in order to buy tokens. He was not eligible for Fuel Direct. His family, which included two children, used gas for cooking, heating and hot water. They had bought a bottled gas room heater and hot plate. They boiled a kettle on the hot plate for hot water.

Percy was annoyed that his offer of £20 towards his payment plan had been rejected before disconnection. He could not afford to pay the whole bill and so made an appointment to be disconnected. He was enfuriated when the engineers came to disconnect him a day early. Percy was determined not to get in touch again.

Len also got in touch before disconnection to try and explain his situation, but was still disconnected. He felt that, apart from disconnection, his situation had not changed and so any further contact would be equally unsuccessful. He was now waiting to go to court to try and get his gas reconnected. Len already had direct deductions for water and poll tax and did not want any more money taken out of his benefit. He was not aware that he might be able to have a token meter and certainly did not remember being offered one before disconnection. Although he was very dependent on gas (for heating and cooking) and the winter was drawing in, Len was living on his own and felt he could cope without his gas supply.

Fraser was in dispute over estimated bills and, although he had enough money to pay his bill, was determined not to do so. He was unsuccessful in solving the problem before disconnection and now had more faith in the courts to solve it.

Mohammed actually did get in touch with British Gas immediately after disconnection to try and arrange reconnection but was so upset by the way he had been treated that he did not feel there was any point in making further contact. Mohammed was angry that he had been given no alternative but to pay his arrears and his new bill before reconnection. He bought an electric cooker and tried to live without gas. He eventually saved up enough money and his anger abated so that he could arrange to be reconnected.

Living without gas

For these people, then, it was a question of living without their gas supply. It was clear that in some instances this was causing considerable hardship. The experience of disconnection was often quite traumatic. The subsequent experience of living without gas was often equally difficult to cope with, even for a short period of time. Many of those disconnected were out of work and so were probably more dependent on gas as they spent more time at home. People in the study were interviewed between July and October, so lack of heating was not generally a problem at this time.

Sid did not have enough money to pay the whole bill and so was disconnected. He said he:

> *Just lived on toast. The bairns took me out two or three times a week to have some dinner ... I had to boil kettles and strip off and have a good wash in the sink.*

Living without gas for more than a month or two caused emotional as well as practical difficulties. In London, John did not know his neighbours, and so could not rely on them for help. Since disconnection, he had been without any cooking or hot water facilities – he did not even have an electric kettle. His only source of warmth was a coal fire in the lounge. He sometimes ate out, but could not afford this very often and generally felt that he was not eating very healthily. He went to the public baths when he needed to wash, but again this cost money.

Len was interviewed late in October and it had already begun to snow in Rotherham. He had been unemployed for 14 years and was dependent on gas for heating, hot water and cooking facilities. At the time of the interview, he had been disconnected for almost three months. Len managed by spending as much time as possible outside the house. After 14 years of unsuccessful jobsearch, he still spent a lot of time looking for work (and quite a lot of his money went on bus fares). He also went walking in the woods to pass the time. When he wanted a bath, he went to his sister and his neighbour sometimes cooked for him and washed some of his clothes. He ate out occasionally, but knew that this was expensive. Len felt that he was treated as a third class citizen because he was poor.

Part III
CONCLUSIONS

19 Conclusions

This study set out to discover the reasons why a large proportion of people had no contact with British Gas prior to being disconnected for arrears on their gas bills. Official statistics suggested that, in the last quarter of 1992, 62 per cent of people who were disconnected from their gas supply had had no contact before disconnection. Moreover, there were wide regional variations in this figure, ranging from 54 per cent in North Thames to 95 per cent in the North East.

It soon became clear that these statistics fail to tell the whole story. In many cases that had been categorised as having no contact, customers had, in fact, been in touch with British Gas – by letter, telephone and personal visit – and often people had made offers of part payment. What we do not know for certain is whether this contact went unrecorded or whether the definitions used for creating the statistics lead to an understatement of the level of contact between British Gas and its customers. It seems most likely that both explanations were true.

We have, therefore, concentrated on understanding why people get into arrears with their bills and why at least 15,000 people a year end up disconnected from their gas supply despite British Gas's intentions that disconnection should be a last resort when all other avenues have failed.

Arrears recovery and low income households

One of the most striking findings of the research is the very low incomes that the majority of families were living on. In particular, nearly a quarter of families had incomes that were below the level of Income Support.

There were a number of ways that low incomes, often in combination with other factors, had contributed to people's debt problems. Hardly any of these are specific to problems paying gas bills and call for more wide-ranging solutions related to the payment of social security.

First, those who live long-term on social security have few reserves to fall back on to meet large quarterly fuel bills or unexpected expenditure. This might involve relatively large sums of money, such as buying curtains, floor covering and meeting other costs of an enforced house move, but could be for much more modest amounts, like replacing a television aeriel. Others had received unexpectedly large gas bills after moving into a new home. Occurrences such as these were usually enough to disrupt the household budget and lead to arrears that could not be repaid. The social fund cannot help people facing problems with quarterly fuel bills. In theory, it should help cushion people against some of the unexpected costs by providing interest-free loans, but in practice this had not helped. This provides still more evidence that the policy for assisting long-term claimants to meet 'lumpy' expenditure needs to be reviewed.

Secondly, debarring people from benefit if 'voluntarily unemployed' may need review. The introduction of 'hardship payments', that is, reduced Income Support payments, may be better than nothing, but these payments usually *exacerbated* or *led to* hardship rather than reduced or avoided it. Two of the three people who had received hardship payments had not given up their jobs voluntarily. Sid had been made redundant and received hardship payments while his claim for Unemployment Benefit was calculated; John had been persuaded to give up work on health grounds. Given the very low payments these men received, financial problems seem inevitable, making it all the more important that people should not lightly be debarred from benefits.

Thirdly, there is the question of unclaimed social security. The debate on benefit take-up usually focusses on the proportion of people who are eligible for benefit but for one reason or another fail to claim. Less often is there consideration of the consequences of not claiming for the individuals concerned. This study shows those consequences all too clearly. The benefit which stood out above all others in this regard was Family Credit, a tax-free benefit for workers with children. The take-up rate for Family Credit is estimated at between 60 and 65 per cent. Moreover, it is argued that many of those not claiming would, in any case, be entitled to only small sums of money and that they, presumably, do not feel it worthwhile to claim. Six of the 48 families were not claiming their Family Credit entitlement, and a further two had been in that position in the recent past. For these families it was not a question of a few pounds unclaimed. The amounts varied between £24 and £84 a week. All but one of them were in debt, many of them with debts besides their gas arrears. This confirms a recent study of mortgage arrears which also found significant under-claiming of Family Credit (Ford and Wilcox, 1992).

While we have highlighted specific changes to the social security system, another way of helping many people on low incomes would be to address the issue of capital investment in housing stock. Brenda Boardman argues that, 'fuel poverty is the inability to afford adequate warmth due to the energy inefficiency of the home'. While the issue of energy inefficiency was not central to this research, it is important to note Boardman's conclusions that capital investment, rather than raising benefit levels would be a more cost effective and environmentally sound way of tackling the problem of fuel poverty (Boardman, 1991). We agree broadly with this conclusion, but would argue that such investment would not solve the problems of long-term benefit claiming, hardship payments and non take-up of benefit. While capital investment may significantly reduce fuel poverty, other measures are also necessary.

The primary responsibility for tackling the problems of low income rests not with the utilities but with the government. But it seems unjust that families in these circumstances should be further penalised by having their gas, electricity or water disconnected. There are a number of steps that British Gas and other utilities might take to help people on low incomes.

One of the first steps must be to encourage people to make contact if they have problems paying a gas bill. Many had failed to do so, chiefly because they believed that they had to pay their arrears in full and did not have the money to do so. This view seemed to be reinforced by the messages they received early in the debt recovery procedure. Alternative payment methods are spelt out in full only in the *Helpline Pack*, which seemed to arrive too late for people to negotiate payment plans, Fuel Direct or a prepayment meter and so avoid disconnection. Some people had, it seemed, not received the *Helpline Pack* at all. While it may be that only a very small fraction of debtors do not receive the pack, these people may have a much higher risk of disconnection. There is, therefore, a need to make sure that everyone in default is made aware of the alternative payment methods.

Secondly, some people had tried to establish contact and to explain their circumstances, even if some of these approaches were somewhat tentative. This contact went unrecorded, and offers to pay failed to prevent disconnection. It is British Gas's intention that they 'will ensure that customers with payment difficulties who make contact with appropriate staff will receive sympathetic treatment at all times'. For a variety of reasons this seems not to have been the reality for a number of people. Part of the solution must lie with staff training. There are a number of areas that could usefully be covered by this training: awareness of the sorts of circumstance that this study has shown to be associated with arrears; dealing with people who are suffering from stress and anxiety following job loss, business failure or relationship breakdown; and communicating with people for whom English is a second language.

For those where there is contact, the first means of recovering arrears is through a negotiated repayment plan. Of course many of these are successful in avoiding disconnection, whilst ensuring that owed money is paid. In other instances such plans break down and lead to disconnection. Officially these are recorded as 'broken contact'; in practice broken payment plan is a more appropriate description, since a number of people had contacted British Gas about their difficulties keeping to the agreed plan. In some cases the repayment plan they had agreed to was unrealistic, given their circumstances. This suggests a need to consider the financial circumstances of customers and set a realistic level of repayment of arrears. The frequency of payment also needs to match the frequency with which they receive their income. At the same time people should be encouraged to inform British Gas of any changes to their circumstances which make it difficult to pay so that the repayment plan can be renegotiated.

Other repayment plans, set up by elderly or disabled people, had been disrupted by mobility problems making it difficult for them to get to a gas showroom. A wider range of payment points, perhaps through local post offices, might help overcome this problem.

Not everyone wants a fixed weekly payment plan. Those on low incomes and who were the most careful budgeters preferred to retain as much control over their finances as possible. More flexible payment arrangements would be best suited to their needs, allowing them to repay the bill in as short a time as possible. Unfortunately some arrangements of this type were not confirmed in writing and people who were fully prepared to pay the bill in instalments were disconnected.

For social security claimants, provision exists for fuel bill arrears to be deducted at source from their benefit payments, a system known as 'Fuel Direct'. There was evidence that this procedure was not always working as intended. In particular, there is a need to inform people much earlier on about the availability of Fuel Direct.

Discussions with the Department of Social Security are needed on a number of issues. Ways need to be explored to ensure that people do not get disconnected whilst fixing up direct payments. Possible solutions include speeding up the application process or liaising more effectively with British Gas when a request has been made for Fuel Direct. Local staff should not be telling claimants that fuel direct is available only after disconnection. Steps should be taken to ensure that people in multiple debt do not voluntarily agree to unrealistic deductions that leave them with far too little to live on. Finally, there are problems when people cease to be eligible for Fuel Direct, but still live on a low income. A smooth transition from Fuel Direct to a payment plan would help in such cases.

In the longer term, consideration might be given to the practicalities of Fuel Direct being used to enable all social security claimants without a bank account to set up a prepayment plan in order to avoid future arrears.

The last line of defence before disconnection is the installation of a prepayment token meter. Technical problems have prevented a suitable meter being developed as quickly for gas as for electricity payments. As a consequence, availability of meters has been restricted to people who have gas arrears and face disconnection. This has led to a situation where some people build up sizeable arrears before they can get the payment method of their choice. As soon as meter supply problems have been resolved, prepayment meters should be offered to all those who would choose to pay this way.

A number of people were resistant to the possibility of paying for their gas by token meter. There were a number of reasons for this. First, there were practical considerations. Most commonly these related to the cost and time involved in getting tokens. Secondly there were attitudes to money management. It seems that those most attracted to token meters are the minority of people who like to keep a very close watch on their finances. The majority, who find the constant preoccupation with money a burden, would prefer to pay by direct debit – from bank accounts if they have them or from social security benefit if they qualify for direct deductions. In such circumstances it seems that low-income families who decline a meter have little option but to face disconnection. Further research may be required to give a more detailed understanding of the resistance to token meters.

Again, as with Fuel Direct, people are finding out about meters too late to prevent disconnection, and need to be told about them much earlier in the debt-recovery process. Others may be refused a prepayment meter until they have repaid all their arrears. This seems to run counter to British Gas policy.

There are also practical problems with prepayment meters. The cost and inconvenience of travel to get tokens; the fact that post offices will sell £1 tokens only in batches of five; high levels of calibration and linking the rate of debt repayment to current consumption are all contributing to a problem of 'self-disconnection' whereby people cannot afford to keep themselves warm.

Prior to disconnection, it is standard practice for British Gas to notify the local authority social services department of the names and addresses of the families involved. There was no evidence that this information had been acted on to avoid disconnection, even though social workers were involved with some of the families we interviewed. This procedure requires review, involving discussions with staff of social services departments.

Welfare rights officers should be involved in these discussions to try to find ways of identifying those families not receiving benefit they are entitled to claim.

Arrears recovery and other households

Higher income households mostly get into difficulties either because they are away from home or because they are disorganised about budgeting and bill paying. Payment plans, using standing orders or direct debit, would overcome these problems. Customers with bank accounts should be encouraged to pay in this way and be sent the necessary forms to set up the arrangement.

But this is not the end of the story. There were instances where standing order problems had caused the debt in the first place. Where this is the case, customers need to be told immediately; and any communications should look different from the usual statements they receive when the standing order is working.

Disconnection

In view of the strong link between poverty and gas disconnection it seems a particularly harsh sanction for many who fail to pay their gas bills. This point has been made before (Berthoud, 1981) and a suggestion made that automatic installation of a prepayment meter should replace disconnection as the ultimate penalty for gas bill arrears. This suggestion is not itself without problems, given the difficulties that arise for some people paying by prepayment meter. Even so, alternatives to disconnection merit detailed consideration.

At all income levels estimated bills cropped up as a recurrent problem. Indeed one person had been disconnected because he was no longer willing to pay any money following an unresolved dispute over estimated bills. In July 1992, the 1986 Gas Act was amended so that a gas supplier is no longer entitled to disconnect for any amount that is 'genuinely in dispute'.

The disconnection process was clearly traumatic for the people concerned, with a common feeling of violation akin to burglary. Entry without permission should be undertaken only as a last resort, yet there was an instance of a date being fixed for disconnection but being brought forward without notifying the customer.

Many of those who are disconnected contact British Gas soon after disconnection. They report a change in the way that they are received by staff and often find them unhelpful. The anger and frustration felt by those who have been disconnected will not be conducive to negotiation of repayment and reconnection and staff must often be as bruised by this experience as the customers. Staff who deal with customers who have been disconnected need training in understanding and diffusing their emotions.

Reconnection

For very low income households, the reconnection fee can be the last straw. Where financial circumstances justify it, reconnection fees should be waived.

British Gas statistics

This study was prompted by concern about high levels of non-contact among households who are disconnected for not having paid their gas bill. It has shown, however, that the problem of disconnection is a much more complex one, requiring a number of different solutions. This needs to be reflected in the way that cases are categorised for statistical purposes so that the figures give a more accurate picture of the disconnection problem.

Prognosis

British Gas's concern about the level of disconnections cannot be doubted; nor can their determination to tackle the problem. Commissioning this research was an important first step down this road.

Bibliography

Berthoud, *Fuel Debts and Hardship*, PSI, 1981

Berthoud and Kempson, *Credit and Debt*, PSI, 1992

Boardman, *Fuel Poverty*, Belhaven Press, 1991

Community Energy Research and Birmingham Settlement, *Hidden Disconnections*, JRF, 1993

Daniel, *The Unemployed Flow*, PSI, 1990

Ford and Wilcox, *Mortgage Arrears*, 1992

Kempson, Bryson and Rowlingson, *Ends that Won't Meet*, PSI, 1993, forthcoming

Marsh and McKay, *Families, Work and Benefits*, PSI, 1993, forthcoming

SCPR, *Code of Practice Payment Arrangements*, 1983

Yu, *Low Cost Budget Standards for Three Household Types*, University of York, Family Budgets Unit, 1992

Appendix 1

Technical report

Sample

The sample was provided by British Gas according to PSI's specifications. Three British Gas regions were sampled (Northern, East Midlands and North Thames) and quotas were set on four contact categories.

Fieldwork

A letter on PSI headed paper was sent to all customers in the sample informing them of the study and asking them to opt out of the study using the enclosed prepaid envelope if they did not wish to take part. Several letters were received by PSI, but all actually requested interviews rather than refused. One of those who wrote in was subsequently interviewed.

Karen Rowlingson conducted a pilot exercise to test the topic guide and the contacting procedure. Interviewers were then briefed at the beginning of the mainstage on 6 August 1992. Fieldwork began immediately after the briefing and continued until 18 November 1992. This fairly long fieldwork period enabled us to contact some people who may be away for a month or two at a time. The interviewers who worked on the study were Jane Malone and Jan Lecluse in North Thames, Chris Jacobs in East Midlands and Jill Hearn in Northern.

Virtually all the contacting was conducted in person by interviewers visiting people's homes. In one or two cases where the address was very distant or several personal contacts had been attempted, interviewers did resort to making contact by telephone (if a telephone number was available).

PSI's contact record

Table 1 shows that 209 addresses were originally sampled, heavily skewed towards North Thames because that region has a higher rate of disconnection and non-contact. The North Thames region stretches from High Wycombe and Ascot in the West to Canvey Island, Southend and Basildon in the East. This is a very large region and so although the 123 original addresses were sampled from the whole region, it was decided to withdraw 33 of these before fieldwork began in order to cluster the addresses more. Having said this, the final sample was still fairly unclustered and included addresses in High Wycombe and Slough as well as more central and East London locations such as Camden, Kensington and Hackney. This ensured that the study included a range of people and, therefore, reasons for disconnection. The addresses in the East Midlands were equally unclustered, ranging from Sheffield and Doncaster to Derby and Leicester. Those in the Northern region were clustered around Newcastle upon Tyne and South Shields.

Table 1   PSI's contact record, by region

	Northern	E.Midlands	N.Thames	Total
Issued	41	45	123	209
Removed from sample (too far)	0	0	33	33
Not visited, quota full	0	18	28	46
Abandoned, quota full	3	13	18	34
Can't find address	4	0	2	6
Moved out	10	2	4	16
Away for long time	3	1	6	10
Refused	5	1	5	11
Broken appointment	3	0	3	6
Duplicate address	0	0	1	1
Language difficulties	0	0	1	1
Successful	13	10	22	45

Quotas were set on different categories in order to look at different types of contact and non-contact at various stages. The first category was 'broken contact'. Although PSI ideally wanted to include all examples of broken contact (for example, someone who gets in touch because they have a problem and then still gets disconnected), British Gas records are not able to categorise people in this way. Category 1 therefore comprises those who have a problem, make a payment plan and are subsequently disconnected. Category 2 comprises customers who have set up a payment plan and have not been disconnected. Category 3 comprises people who did not get in touch before disconnection, but who did so within two weeks afterwards. Category 4 comprises people who got in touch neither before nor within two weeks after disconnection. These categories are normally used by

British Gas to give overall figures on the number of broken contact cases, post-disconnection contact and post-disconnection non-contact.

Table 2 gives the outcome of all the addresses sampled, by category type.

Table 2   PSI's contact record, by category type

	Category				Total
	1 Broken contact	2 Payment plans	3 Pre-discon. non-contact	4 Post-discon. non-contact	
Issued	35	60	43	71	209
Removed from sample (too far)	1	13	8	11	33
Not visited, quota full	5	15	0	26	46
Abandoned, quota full	3	7	9	11	34
Can't find address	1	2	2	1	6
Moved out	5	1	3	7	16
Away for long time	1	3	3	3	10
Refused	1	6	2	2	11
Broken appt	3	0	3	0	6
Duplicate address	0	0	1	0	1
Language difficulties	0	1	0	0	1
Successful	11	12	12	10	45

When the quotas on the categories were full, 46 addresses had not been visited and 34 had been visited, but no contact had been established. In six cases, it was very difficult to find the address – some were not on street maps. In 16 cases, interviewers gained information from neighbours or rent offices that the people in the sample had permanently left their homes. In 10 cases, interviewers found out that people were away and were expected to be away for a long time. The interviewers received 11 refusals. There were also six broken appointments.

Although this is a small sample, it does seem that those in category 4 are more likely to have moved away or be absent for home for a long time. The fairly small number of refusals (11), is related to the fact that at the beginning of fieldwork several letters were received from respondents, asking to be interviewed as they wished to tell PSI about their experience of disconnection (not all of these were actually interviewed). Willingness to be interviewed was therefore not a problem, but contacting was. The interviewers often had to make repeated calls to addresses at different times of the day and different times of the week before they found people in.

The implications of this are that if British Gas wished to make a serious effort to contact people face-to-face, then they would have to be prepared to make several call-backs. It is unlikely that one visit before disconnection (usually during a weekday in working hours) is going to be successful in finding people in.

Non-contact analysis

Although 33 addresses were removed from the sample before fieldwork and a further 54 were never visited (because quotas had been fulfilled or the address could not be traced), PSI has information on the remaining 124 addresses. Of course, 45 of these were interviewed and so details are included in the report. For those addresses which were visited, but where interviews were not obtained, interviewers were asked to give detailed descriptions about the area and housing condition as well as any other information from neighbours.

Many of the refusals came from people in fairly affluent housing. This ranged from a detached house in an affluent suburb (with a J registration Toyota in the drive), to a small terraced cottage to a well kept terraced house. In three cases a go-between (two daughters and one wife) refused on behalf of the respondent and would not let the interviewer talk directly to the respondent. In most cases, typical reasons were given for refusal - lack of time and interest. In some cases, people were more specific. A couple said they were paying by direct debit and had no problems so could see no point in participating. One person said he was very busy with work and his mother was ill. Another had just come back from holiday to find that the firm he worked for was in trouble. He was also going away to Cyprus the following week.

The number of refusals was fairly low, but it is even more reassuring that most came from people who were on payment plans (category 2) and were (apparently) not having difficulties.

There were many signs of people being away from home (either permanently or temporarily). These were very overgrown gardens, post piling up inside the door, boarded up windows, lights never on even at night and general disrepair. In this section, there was a mixture of housing types, from semi-detached council houses to small terraced cottages to maisonettes. The general quality of this housing was poorer than that for the refusals.

After many trips to a house over several weeks, it becomes apparent whether anyone is living there. Neighbours and, sometimes, new occupiers then confirm or deny this. Many know when the people moved out and some know approximately where they went (one moved 50 miles away, another moved from the North East to Torquay). People in London knew less (or were willing to say less) about their neighbours than in the Midlands and North East.

Those who were away temporarily were sometimes away for three to four months. Some were working abroad (one had gone to work on the oil rigs, another was singing her way around Europe). Others were away on long trips.

The other addresses which were visited but then abandoned because the quota was full also spanned the range of housing types – from cottages in upmarket villages, to semi-detached houses, to maisonettes, to high-rise blocks of flats, to town houses in the red light districts. Generally, accommodation was in a poor state of repair. In London, particularly, there were many flats with entryphone systems making it difficult to see the actual residence of the named contact. Entryphones would also make it difficult for British Gas to contact (for example, in delivering *Helpline Packs*).

Analysis
Tape recordings were made of all but two interviews (due to respondent refusal to be taped). Along with these, interviewers were asked to make very detailed notes about the interview. Using the tapes and notes, charts were drawn up and data entered for each respondent under relevant headings.

Appendix 2

Sample profile

Table 3   Overall income levels of families

	Category				
	1	2	3	4	All
Above average income	2	(1)	4	4	10 (1)
Low wage	1	1 (4)	5	1	8 (4)
not eligible for FC/HB		*1*	*3*		*4*
eligible for FC					
claiming		*(2)*			*(2)*
not claiming	*1*	*(2)*	*2*	*1*	*4 (2)*
Income support	4	2	5	5	16
Other benefit	4	1 (1)			5 (1)
Not claiming IS/UB		2	1		3
Total	11	6 (6)	15*	10	42 (6)

*   includes 3 extra families in the Khan household

Figures in brackets denote those without arrears

Table 4   Age profile of customers

	Arrears n=38*	Disconn. n=32*	Credit & debt %	GHS %
Age				
under 29	8	5	32	12
30-39	8	8	30	
40-49	13	12	21	} 52
50-59	5	4	8	
60-69	3	2	7	17
70 and over	1	1	2	18

* excludes one household where the landlord was a gas customer

Table 5   Type of household

	Arrears n=38*	Disconn. n=32*	Credit & debt %	GHS %
Pensioner	2	1	6	16
Single person	10	10	24	9
Couple no kids	4	2	14	27
Couple with kids	8	8	37	26
Lone parent	8	5	19	5
Other adult households	6	6	-	17

* excludes one household where the landlord was the gas customer

Table 6   Ethnic origin of customers

	Arrears n=38*	Disconn. n=32*	GHS %
White British	29	23	95
Asian	3	3	2
Afro-caribbean	3	3	1
Others	3	3	2

*   excludes one household where the landlord was the gas customer

Table 7   Household type by income level

	On benefit or ENC	Low wage	Above average	All
Pensioner (16%)	2			2
Single person (9%)	8		2	10
Couple no kids (27%)	2	2		4
Couple with kids (26%)	3	3	2	8
Lone parent (5%)	5	1	2	8
Other adult households (17%)	1	1	4	6
plus the Khan family	(2)	(2)		

Base: Those with arrears (38 households; 42 families)

British Gas figures

Table 8   British Gas contact figures for quarter ending December 1992

	Total	N.Thames	E.Midlands	Northern
Customers	17.0m	1.9m	1.7m	0.9m
Meters installed during quarter*	37,261 0.2%	2,968 0.2%	3,565 0.2%	1,571 0.2%
Payment arrangements made during quarter*	208,804 1.3%	2,857 0.2%	45,474 2.7%	0*** 0%***
Fuel Direct arrangements*	216,024 1.3%	23,634 1.2%	21,098 1.2%	19,906 2.2%
Disconnections*	3,926 0.02%	1,185 0.06%	428 0.03%	164 0.02%
No-contact at all**	2,443 62%	643 54%	267 62%	155 95%
Broken contact after failure of payment plan**	1,334 34%	527 44%	144 34%	3 2%
Reconnections within one month**	877 20%	195 15%	122 25%	30 15%

*   Percentages based on total number of customers

**   Percentages based on total number of disconnections

*** In British Gas Northern, all payment arrangements operate under the Gas Payment Plan so payment arrangements do not appear in these statistics.